The Little Book of
of
CAMPAIGN
Étiquette

The Little Book of

CAMPAIGN Etiquette

FOR EVERYONE WITH A STAKE IN POLITICIANS AND JOURNALISTS

STEPHEN HESS

INTRODUCTION BY
Judith Martin

BROOKINGS INSTITUTION PRESS
Washington, D.C.

Copyright © 1998 by

THE BROOKINGS INSTITUTION
1775 Massachusetts Avenue, N.W.
Washington, D.C. 20036

Introduction copyright © 1998 by Judith Martin

Library of Congress Cataloging-in-Publication data

Hess, Stephen.
    The little book of campaign etiquette : for everyone with a
stake in politicians and journalists / by Stephen Hess.
    p. cm.
    Includes bibliographical references and index.
    ISBN 0-8157-3586-3 (cloth : alk. paper)
    1. Electioneering—United States.   2. Government
etiquette—United States.   3. Political ethics—United States.   I. Title.
    JK2281 .H49 1998
    395.5—ddc21   98-25365
                                              CIP

9 8 7 6 5 4 3 2 1

The paper used in this publication meets the minimum requirements of the American
National Standard for Information Sciences—Permanence of Paper for Printed
Library Materials, ANSI Z39.48-1984

Typeset in Minion and Minion Expert

Composition by R. Lynn Rivenbark, Macon, Georgia

Printed by R. R. Donnelley and Sons, Harrisonburg, Virginia

For Nathaniel Cody Hess
on his first birthday

Acknowledgments

THIS BOOK grew out of conversations with Paul C. Light, part of whose mandate as Director of the Public Policy Program at the Pew Charitable Trusts is to worry about Americans' increasing disengagement from the ordinary events of democratic life, chief among them elections. What Dr. Light saw the need for was a set of clearly understood rules of engagement against which to hold accountable the candidates and the journalists who report on the candidates.

Our proposal for a simple set of norms against which to measure campaign conduct was supported by the board of The Pew Charitable Trusts and resulted in a major grant in 1996. Other funding was provided by the Deer Creek Foundation and the Cissy Patterson Trust.

Our conversations were enthusiastically supported by Pew's president, Rebecca W. Rimal, and resulted in a major grant in 1996. Other funding was provided by the Deer Creek Foundation and the Cissy Patterson Trust.

These essays were aided by three roundtables at Brookings whose participants were William C. Adams, Elizabeth Arnold, Dan Balz, Richard L. Berke, Christine Black, Adam Clymer, Everette Dennis, E. J. Dionne Jr., Ronald Elving, Curtis B. Gans, Cragg Hines, Ellen Hume, Gwen Ifill,

The Little Book of Campaign Etiquette

Maxine Isaacs, Andrew Kohut, Carl P. Leubsdorf, Thomas E. Mann, Stuart Rothenberg, Paul Taylor, and John Yang.

The manuscript then benefited from the critiques of Christopher Arterton, Barbara Cochran, E. J. Dionne Jr., Maxine Isaacs, Marvin Kalb, Thomas Mann, Tom Rosenstiel, and Paul Taylor.

A special thanks to the inspired cartoonists who contributed their work to this book: Clay Bennett, Steve Benson, Charles Bissell, Herbert Block, Jim Borgman, John Branch, Gary Brookins, Paul Conrad, Charlie Daniel, Mark Fiore, Bob Gorrell, Walt Handelsman, John Kovalic, Mike Luckovich, Jeff MacNelly, Jimmy Margulies, Mike Peters, Joel Pett, Rob Rogers, Wayne Stayskal, Stephen Templeton, Tom Toles, Garry Trudeau, Dan Wasserman, Don Wright; and to the Political Communication Center at the University of Oklahoma for the photographs of the Willie Horton commercial.

Thanks also to the editors of *The Harvard International Journal of Press/Politics* and the Knight Ridder Newspapers, where some of this material previously appeared.

The book was hatched in the Governmental Studies Program at Brookings: Thomas Mann, director, and Robert A. Katzmann, acting director, 1998. Patricia Fowlkes provided personal and technical assistance; Susan Stewart, Judy Light, and Kristen Lippert-Martin provided support assistance; Lawson Rollins and Laurel Imig provided research assistance, as did intern Lara C. Rusch. Jim Schneider edited the manuscript and Carlotta Ribar proofread the pages.

Once again my deep appreciation to Michael H. Armacost, President of the Brookings Institution, the trustees, and fellow members of the staff, good colleagues and friends, none of whom, of course, need subscribe to any of these views on campaign etiquette.

July 1998   S.H.
Washington, D.C.

Contents

Introduction
Judith Martin

IT IS AN HONOR, not to mention a mercy, to welcome Stephen Hess to the noble profession of telling people to cut that out right this minute if they know what's good for them and start behaving like civilized human beings. In this century, etiquette has not received the philosophical and practical attention to which it had been accustomed since civilization began, and the need is getting more acute by the minute.

Everyone is now screaming for civility. Of course if everyone would stop screaming, we might have it. Civility is one social blessing that does not require funding.

Our Founding Fathers were deeply interested in the task of adapting European etiquette, riddled as it was with court ritual and class distinctions, to an egalitarian society. That they failed to come up with the insouciant twentieth century notion of just abolishing etiquette altogether was not because they lacked interest in liberty, never noticed that the freedom of the individual might be in conflict with the welfare of the community, or were so hidebound by tradition that they never dared to attempt revolutionary change.

Rather, they seemed to have taken it for granted that forms are necessary to avert conflicts and to thrash out differences, and that extralegal rules protect even the most obnoxious individuals more than regulating every small or personal problem with the full force of law.

That lesson is now painfully being learned. When it came to be thought that any self-restraint was too high a price to pay for community harmony, the society tried to live by law alone. It soon found itself ricocheting between abrasive living conditions and clumsy legal intrusions into delicate or trivial matters.

Rudeness is not a modern invention, as those overburdened with nostalgia would lead us to believe. People have always behaved badly, which is why rules exist and why social disapproval was exercised to enforce them. What is new in our time is that rudeness has been morally glamorized.

Nowhere has that been more apparent than in the public arena. In politics and journalism it has been considered both dashing and idealistic to cast all niceties aside in order to do the public business properly.

In politics, etiquette has been treated as such a sissy restraint on virtue that obeying it must be a sign of moral turpitude and defying it a sign of moral fervor. A way of demonstrating that one is passionate about one's beliefs would therefore be to scorn to contaminate them through civility to those who differ. Journalism has become one of the most visible professions to subscribe to the idea that etiquette hampers zealous devotion to one's calling and must therefore be suspended so that the profession's sacred obligation to the public can be met.

To be sure, the resulting behavior yielded advantages in the short run. But it was a short run, and it is now over. Those whom rudeness startled or swayed have become aware of the damage it caused. Although members of the public are the supposed beneficiaries of bad behavior among the powerful, they have now turned skeptical and contemptuous of their benefactors.

Perhaps it is because they noticed the catch: our system of government being based on cooperation and compromise, it is difficult to do business in a state of open combat. Our information system being based on encouraging people to air views and issues, it is necessary to hear what people are saying. When everyone is busy posturing and exchanging insults, it becomes impossible to discuss differences, much less to settle them.

So it should probably be counted as progress that what everyone is now fighting over is how to bring back civility. What continues to hold things up is the notion that this can be done without the nuisance of having to obey rules of etiquette.

When the U.S. Congress attempted to improve its standard of behavior, the proposed solution was to hold a retreat in which individuals were encouraged to bond as family friends. But even if it had been possible to achieve complete cronyism (the old-fashioned term for politicians' being more interested in one another's welfare than in the competing claims of the different segments of the public they represent), this failed to address the problem.

The problem is not a lack of personal affection for one's opponents— the problem is a lack of proper professional behavior. The goal is not to become private friends who put their differences aside, but to be able to perform the public business that arises out of these differences.

For this, there must be voluntary submission to rules of civil behavior. Here, then, is a rich mix of rules of etiquette and ethics, morals and manners, prudence and fairness—the stuff of civility.

The Little Book
of
CAMPAIGN
Etiquette

Etiquette

WHEN WE peel away the matter of manners, which Emily Post assures us are merely the tools of etiquette, etiquette can be defined as a system of conventional rules that control our social or professional behavior.

"No rule of law . . . decrees that a soup plate should be tilted away from, never toward, the diner . . . but etiquette ordains it and it is obeyed." So says the *Encyclopedia Britannica.*

Today America is in need of an etiquette for political campaigns as waged by politicians and reported by journalists. "Some people think that etiquette is fine for tea parties, but there's no room for it when important political business has to be done," writes Miss Manners® otherwise known as Judith Martin. "That's not true. The more controversy you have, the more etiquette you need. You need rules and order." The missing ingredient in efforts to improve campaign discourse is a set of agreed-upon norms and standards for behavior.

There's a lot that troubles us about how politics is conducted. Scholar Stephen L. Carter is right: "Our public dialogue—our very language—has been debased through the move toward negativity and even hostility, so that, in an argument, the first weapon we reach for is often the most extreme." "If I can make Willie Horton a household name, we'll win the election," said Lee Atwater, George Bush's 1988 campaign manager, foreshadowing the TV commercial that would link a convicted murderer to the Democratic presidential nominee.

There's a lot that troubles us about how politicians are covered. Journalist Lars-Erik Nelson is right: "We don't even need accusations. All we need are loaded, insinuating questions and we can make anybody look guilty." "Does he have a sexually transmitted disease?" asked National Public Radio's Mara Liasson of the president's press secretary at a White House briefing in 1996.

Under what circumstances is a candidate's sex life acceptable grist for the campaign mill? When is it acceptable to discuss an opponent's family? When is it permissible to ask questions about a candidate's medical records and mental health? Lacking an etiquette, such questions are often answered on the basis of political or journalistic exigency—that is, what will make the biggest headline.

This book is arranged alphabetically: *Advertising, Bias, Conventions, Debates, Endorsements, Families, Gender, Health,* and so forth. There are forty-three entries. Each concludes with suggested rules of etiquette. In case I haven't made myself perfectly clear, the essays are illustrated with the etched-in-acid opinions of some of America's most talented editorial cartoonists, who contributed their genius to this undertaking. And for those who wish to delve deeper into a particular topic, there is a reference guide at the end of the book. While my examples will be drawn largely from presidential campaigns, the principles are generally applicable to all campaigns, from those for the White House to the ones for school board. According to the census, there are 513,200 elected officials in the United States. Probably 250,000 people seek elective office each year.

"Politics is never pretty," Marianne Means of the Hearst Newspapers observes, "but surely it need not be this unrelentingly ugly." I agree. I also agree with E. J. Dionne Jr. that "I'm willing to trade a little authenticity for a little courtesy." Yet only at the edges is this a book about civility. My intention is not to propose courtly ways or to get stuffy about what a *Baltimore Sun* columnist of my youth called "The Great Game of Politics." In San Luis Obispo in 1962, as Richard Nixon was making a speech from the observation platform of the last car of his campaign train, a Democratic prankster named Dick Tuck, wearing a trainman's cap, signaled the engineer to pull out of the station and thus left the candidate stranded in mid-sentence. I was on that train as Nixon's speechwriter and I can still laugh at a good joke. Being of the old school, I continue to think politics can and should be fun. Politics in the United States has a long history as entertainment going back to the torchlight parades with marchers wearing oilskin capes to protect themselves from the dripping of kerosene and giant outdoor rallies measured in acres, 10,000 enthusiasts to the acre.

I'm also old enough to be cranky. Why must every two-bit scandal get a *gate* suffix, as in gurugate or nannygate? Why do TV newscasters seldom admit they're wrong? Why should politicians think we are influenced by whom Barbara Streisand endorses for president? Can't debates be more interesting? Can't there be a more sensible calendar of presidential primaries? I readily admit that some of my agenda gets mixed in with the etiquette.

Ultimately, then, this is a how-to book dedicated to the proposition that all of us, including politicians and journalists, prefer abiding by rules to breaking them. The hard part is agreeing on the rules. Let's get started.

Advertising
(for Consumers)

IN THE LAST presidential campaign, according to the most careful estimates, the Clinton forces spent $98.4 million in television advertising, the Dole camp spent $78.2 million, and Ross Perot's TV budget was about $22 million.

"Is there any facet of American politics more urgently claiming national attention than negative campaign advertisements?" asks a University of Virginia scholar in a law review article. Yet how negative are candidates' ads? It depends on how you define negative. The term is used too loosely by many journalists and academics—negative as the opposite of positive, meaning that candidates, rather than stating their own virtues, attack their opponents. Take this Nixon spot from 1972 as a so-called negative ad:

The scene opens with the camera on a formation of toy soldiers. "The McGovern defense plan," says the narrator. "He would cut the Marines by one-third. The Air Force by one-third. He'd cut Navy personnel by one-fourth, He would cut interceptor planes by one-half. The Navy fleet by one-half. . . ." A hand comes across the screen and

sweeps away the toys. "President Nixon doesn't believe we should play
games with our national security."

The size of the defense force is a legitimate issue. The differences
between Richard Nixon and George McGovern were notable. While
hardly playing games, McGovern did propose budget cuts that could be
translated into reductions in personnel and equipment. Should this be
called a negative ad? No, it's an attack ad or a comparison ad.

Kathleen Hall Jamieson and her colleagues at the Annenberg School
of Communication, University of Pennsylvania, appropriately label
commercials as *attack* (the case against an opponent), *advocacy* (self-
promotion), and *comparison* (the difference between candidates). As
Professor William Mayer of Northeastern University points out, "We
need to find out about the candidates' strengths, it is true, but we also
need to learn about their weaknesses: the abilities and virtues they don't
have; the mistakes they have made; the problems they haven't dealt with;
the issues they would prefer not to talk about; the bad or unrealistic policies they have proposed." Jamieson's research finds that comparative ads
are the most useful to voters.

As political consumers let's reserve *negative* for what we once called
dirty—nasty and mean-spirited remarks based on rumors, lies, and
half-truths that too often debase American electioneering. (These were
quaintly called *canards* in nineteenth-century America.) Here's an example. In California in 1993 a remorseless killer named Richard Allen
Davis kidnapped and murdered a twelve-year-old girl, Polly Klaas.
California Congressman Vic Fazio's opponent used computer graphics
to "morph" the face of Davis into the face of Fazio. The ad goes back
and forth between these images of the killer and the congressman. The
facts behind the ad are that Fazio, who voted many times for a federal
death penalty while in the U.S. House of Representatives, had voted

against a death penalty nineteen years earlier when he was in the state legislature.

We turn to the roles of journalists and politicians—see "Advertising (for Journalists)" and "Advertising (for Politicians)"—in sorting out an etiquette for campaign advertising.

Advertising
(for Journalists)

"MR. EISENHOWER, what about the high cost of living?" a woman asks the candidate. He replies, "My wife Mamie worries about the same thing. I tell her it's our job to change that on November 4 [1952]." Thus is born the spot TV commercial in a presidential campaign. (Also in evidence for the first time is the ability of TV political advertising to alter reality: the commercial was made by first recording Eisenhower's "answer" to the question that hadn't been asked.) Nearly 39 percent of American homes then had TV sets.

Cut to 1988. TV advertising is now the voters' most important source of information on candidates. George Bush, running against Michael Dukakis, turns a rapist named Willie Horton into a household name, and TV journalists invent "the ad watch" to measure the truthfulness of a candidate's message.

Too often, however, the ad watch is no more than a recycling of the ad as a news story. The campaign gets a freebie because the ad is shown without serious analysis. Indeed, looking back on the year of the Willie Horton ad, Roger Ailes, Bush's media guru, says, "You get a 30 or 40 percent bump out of getting [your ad] on the news."

Ad watch fact checking tends to examine scripts, with little attention to the truthfulness of the pictures or other components of the commercials. Since the simple splicing days of 1952, video technologies have vastly expanded producers' ability to manipulate material—computerized alterations, audio distortions, repositionings, and digital editing. The techno-tricks in 1992 and 1996 accelerated George Bush's voice in a Pat Buchanan ad, distorted Bush's lips in a Bill Clinton ad, blurred Steve Forbes's image in a Bob Dole ad, and simulated Clinton's voice in a Lamar Alexander ad. Pictures not self-evident to viewers as distortions are clearly designed to be misleading.

Ad watches should tell consumers whether an ad is an honest representation of the situation depicted; if not, how is it distorted? Instead, Kathleen Hall Jamieson concludes, "Too often, reporters focus on campaign strategy rather than the substance of the commercials." Not what the ad says, but why the ad maker wants to say it. In the 1996 presidential campaign 100 percent of the TV networks' ad watches and 70 percent of newspaper ad watches were devoted to strategy analysis.

It takes a lot more time and knowledge to ferret out ads' misleading claims. Unfortunately the sheer quantity of political commercials can overwhelm the resources of the press corps. It is estimated that 750,000 political spots ran in 1996. One solution: in Oklahoma, Professor Lynda Lee Kaid recruited her university colleagues to analyze ads and post their findings on a computer network where they could be downloaded by reporters.

From April through Election Day 1996, the Clinton and Dole campaigns and their parties broadcast 1,397 hours, or 58 days, worth of commercials in the 75 major media markets. In terms of attempting to woo voters, the commercials are the campaigns. Yet analyses of the commercials, as columnist Martin Schram puts it, are "buried back among the truss ads," while the candidates' appearances are the subjects of front-page reporting. Schram's conclusion is, "We should stop covering

TV ads as some lesser appendage of campaigning and start covering them for what . . . they really are: prime-time speeches made directly to a state's or nation's voters."

The number of ad watches in 1996 was way down from 1992—and the number of misleading statements in the commercials was way up. Ad watches deserve to be improved, not abandoned. Media etiquette on political advertising should

—be commensurate with the importance of advertising in campaigns,

GOING NEGATIVE © John Kovalic. Reprinted with permission of John Kovalic. All rights reserved.

—reflect the amount of money that each candidate devotes to advertising,

—scrutinize competing candidates' ads simultaneously,

—be timely, within twenty-four hours of an ad's release,

—focus on a candidate's message rather than its strategic purpose,

—analyze an ad rather than simply repeat it,

—assess the honesty of pictures and sounds as well as the words.

The Little Book of Campaign Etiquette

Advertising
(for Politicians)

❧❦❧

"WEEKEND PRISON PASSES," commercial produced by Larry McCarthy for Americans for Bush, 1988:

> Audio: "Bush and Dukakis on crime. Bush supports the death penalty for first-degree murderers. Dukakis not only opposes the death penalty, he allowed first-degree murderers to have weekend passes from prison. One was Willie Horton, who murdered a boy in a robbery, stabbing him nineteen times. Despite a life sentence, Horton received ten weekend passes from prison. Horton fled, kidnapped a young couple, stabbing the man and repeatedly raping his girlfriend. Weekend prison passes: Dukakis on crime."

"Today the sky is the limit in political advertising with regard to what can be said, what can be promised, what accusations can be made, what lies can be told," Robert Spero has written in *The Duping of the American Voter: Dishonesty and Deception in Presidential Television Advertising*, which was published twelve years before the Willie Horton ad appeared. Clearly, this is an unloved form of free speech. Yet there is something of a watershed in political commercials that we associate with Willie Horton. The 1988 campaign was the tipping point. Since then, ads have been more negative than positive, hammering at opponents' failures. Voters need to know more than a candidate's self-proclaimed virtues. But there are consequences associated with unrelentingly negative campaigns. Attack ads may, for instance, actually depress voting. And the problem goes beyond affecting the atmosphere of elections to distorting the process of governing. Howard Baker recalls, "When I was leader in the Senate and trying to round up votes on a controversial issue, I would have senators say to me, 'Howard, I would like to vote with you, but they would kill me with negative ads the next time I run.'"

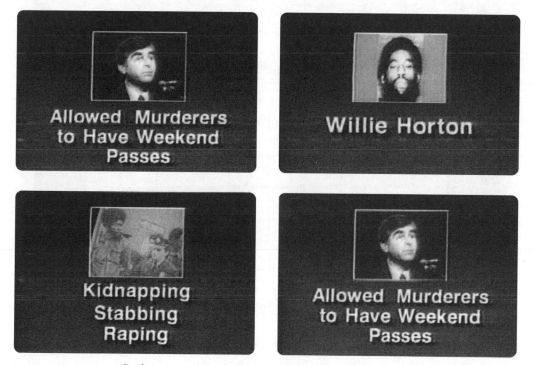

WEEKEND PRISON PASSES, Producer Larry McCarthy for Americans for Bush, 1988. Reprinted with permission of Larry McCarthy. All rights reserved. Photos courtesy of the Political Communication Center, University of Oklahoma.

Another former senator, John Danforth, sees the trend toward the use of negative advertising as changing the decisionmaking process itself, producing "an increasing mood of defensiveness, or testiness, and a breakdown in the comity and collegiality that we need to function as a deliberative body."

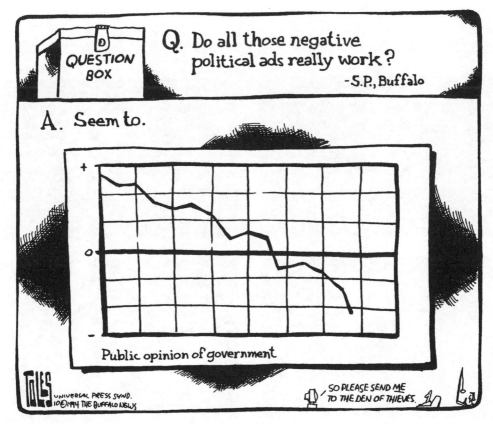

What to do? Here are two routes to develop a campaign etiquette for political advertising.

The Legislative Route. Two members of the U.S. House of Representatives, David Price (D-N.C.) and Steve Horn (R-Calif.), both of whom are also political science professors, want a "Stand By Your Ad" law to hold candidates more accountable for their advertising. The proposal requires candidates and representatives of political parties and independent committees to appear in their radio and TV spots to tell us who they are and that they stand behind the ad's contents. On every TV campaign commercial, for instance, we would see a full-screen view of the candidate stating, "I am [name of candidate], a candidate for [name of office], and I sponsored this advertisement." Similar bills are being introduced in state legislatures. "If candidates are held more accountable for their ads, they'll be less likely to sling mud and more inclined to talk about the issues," says Congressman Price.

The Voluntary Route. On August 6, 1996, in Skowhegan, Maine, seven of the state's ten candidates for U.S. Congress helped draft and then signed a code of ethics. The other three signed soon after. The code is based on the principles of "honesty, fairness, respect for my opponent, responsibility, and compassion." The values are fleshed out with specifics, such as "I shall not use or agree to let third parties use subtle deceptions, half-truths, falsifications. . . . Factual claims made by my campaign will be supported by publicly available documents provided by my campaign office. . . . I shall avoid demeaning references to my opponent and demeaning visual images of my opponent." Many organizations have tried to bind candidates to codes of conduct. What is special about Maine's exercise is the three sponsoring organizations get the candidates themselves to participate in devising the standards.

Anonymous Sources

A FRONT PAGE article in the *New York Times* on September 12, 1987, reported that Senator Joseph Biden, a candidate for the Democratic presidential nomination, had taken a speech by British Labour Party leader Neil Kinnock as his closing statement during a debate at the Iowa State Fair—and, as the article noted, "without crediting Kinnock." The story of Biden's plagiarism, which led to his withdrawal from the race, came from an anonymous source, that is, a person not named in the story. The anonymous source was the campaign manager of a rival candidate.

Among journalists and politicians there is some confusion between the definition of *anonymous source* and *leak*. All leaks are from anonymous sources but not all anonymous sources are leaking. This is because leaks usually refer to previously unrevealed information—grand jury testimony or documents or a public figure's intentions—while anonymous sources may be pedaling opinion, rumor, and gossip. Most journalists view leaks as sacred; anonymous sourcing, however, is often a bad habit.

Do consumers have any right to know where the journalists' information comes from? (As in the Biden-Kinnock example, the origins of the story may be as interesting as the story.) According to a 1985

American Society of Newspaper Editors survey, 49 percent of journalists approve of using unnamed sources, but this approval is only shared by 28 percent of readers.

James Fallows writes in *Breaking the News,* "Under the existing rules of sourcing, reporters can't begin a story by saying: 'The president's campaign manager called me today and, while shielding himself by saying, "This is on deep background," planted rumors about his opponent that he and I both know are untrue.' "

One way for reporters to deal with the problems posed by using anonymous sources, in the opinion of former senator Alan Simpson, is to abandon anonymous source references. "In these cynical times," he adds, "the American people often believe those anonymous sources are you."

News organizations are aware of the validity of Simpson's complaint. The *Washington Post*'s stylebook says that its reporters must "disclose the source of all information when at all possible." The paper's position is that "named sources are vastly to be preferred to anonymous sources. . . . Every time we ask readers to trust an anonymous source, we are putting our credibility on the line. We should always assume that information provided by confidential informants is weaker than information attributable to real people."

Still, according to the *Post*'s ombudsman, Geneva Overholser, "The use of unnamed sources is among American newspapers' most damaging habits. And the *Post* is one of the greatest offenders." She claims the situation has worsened in the past twenty-five years. "The use of anonymous sources has become even more acceptable" in journalism, while "readers have less ability now to judge the source of information."

Based on suggestions of Overholser and others, notably A. H. Raskin in a 1983 report to the National News Council, here are some sensible rules of etiquette for dealing with this problem:

—Reporters should work hard to get information on the record. They should not offer anonymity, but rather should make their sources demand it.

—Anonymous sources should be used only if they are critical to the story and only if the story is of more than ordinary importance.

—Reporters should always explain to readers what an anonymous source's interests are in the story.

—If a source must be anonymous, the reporter has a greater than normal responsibility to make sure that the information is accurate.

Reprinted with permission of Mark Fiore. All rights reserved.

Bias

OUR JUDGMENTS of whether the media are biased ultimately depend on our own biases. Studies have shown that we evaluate the news as being systematically biased against what we believe to be true. Liberals consider the media conservative. Conservatives consider the media liberal.

An organization known as FAIR (Fairness & Accuracy in Reporting) accuses the press of a conservative bias. An organization known as AIM (Accuracy In Media) accuses the press of a liberal bias. Both are right, of course. According to their lights. Press bias is further complicated by the generally accepted proposition that publishers are conservative and reporters are liberal.

Still, can't we calculate a bias that is beyond the eye of the beholder? The newest and most massive survey of American journalists, published in 1996, finds that 44 percent lean Democratic and 16 percent lean Republican. Pushing against the reporters' ideological biases are the traditional norms of "objective" reporting. The vast majority of political reporting is neutral in tone. Yet just as in George Orwell's *Animal Farm,* where all animals are equal but some are more equal than others, a study of five presidential elections concludes, "In sum, the media do not usually favor one candidate, but the candidates they do favor are usually Democrats."

The public's perception is of a press with a bias more often liberal than conservative. A substantial 1996 survey finds 29 percent of Americans think the media tilt left, 13 percent think they tilt right. The public's impression is neither irrelevant nor good for the news business.

While outside groups play a part in exposing press bias, the most effective monitoring of bias must come from journalists themselves. The two finest political reporters I have known in forty years of observing Washington journalists are Alan Otten of the *Wall Street Journal* and David Broder of the *Washington Post,* who practice an etiquette they call "leaning," meaning that when covering a campaign, they deliberately "lean" a little against the candidate they might be inclined to favor. Whatever the etiquette used, it is the awareness that makes the difference. It is the knowledge that bias that may be inadvertent is nonetheless bias.

Muddle America / *Gorrell & Brookins*

Conflict of Interest

"THE SPECTER of 'conflict of interest,'" Michael Kinsley has commented, "arises whenever an individual or institution is involved with more than one goal or person or institution at the same time." He then adds, "This happens to cover a great deal of modern life." Especially for journalists.

For George Will, syndicated newspaper columnist and regular participant on ABC's *This Week with David Brinkley* in 1996, the potential for a conflict of interest was created when his wife became the communications director of Bob Dole's campaign for the Republican nomination. (No stranger to conflict situations, Will in 1980 helped Ronald Reagan prepare for his televised debate with Jimmy Carter.)

For Chuck Scarborough, news anchor on WNBC in New York, the conflict of interest in 1996 was created by his contributing $1,000 each to the campaigns of Dole and Steve Forbes and the revelation that he had made a similar gift to George Bush in 1992 ($1,000 is the maximum allowed by law.)

George Will handled the 1996 potential conflict to his own satisfaction by mentioning his wife's connection to the Dole campaign occasionally (but not routinely), as in a February 4 column: "Dole refused a challenge to sign, there on stage, a no-new-taxes pledge. Mari Maseng, his press secretary then (she now is his campaign communications director and also wife of this columnist, and had a role in Dole's speech responding to the State of the Union), says he refused because . . ."

Neither ABC nor Will's newspaper syndicate, the Washington Post Writers Group, expressed concern. "I don't really want to get into that" (an ABC spokeswoman). "We all have professional spouses. We can't control what they do" (a syndicate spokesman). The *New York Daily News,* however, dropped Will's column for nearly a year because of his involvement in the 1980 Reagan-Carter debate. Scarborough's employer did express regret and barred him from any "original reporting" of politics during the 1996 campaign.

The two journalists represent different aspects of their business. Will is paid to be a purveyor of opinions. Scarborough is paid to keep opinions to himself. Will, as such, considers himself outside the bounds of potential conflict of interest and makes light of those who question his ethics. In response to a critic from *Time,* he writes of three possible solutions: "Mari could quit her career, I could quit mine, or we could get divorced . . . perhaps *Time* should choose."

Will's situation is what Kinsley calls a *confluence of interest.* His opinions have roots and a history; they are not the result of his wife's work, regardless of appearance, and should not present a problem to the attentive political consumer. Scarborough's donation, however, presents a real conflict of interest. As TV critic Eric Mink observed, "Alas, it has become virtually impossible for viewers to watch Scarborough even read a political story from the TelePrompTer without looking for subtle signs of bias in what he says and how he says it. This puts Ch. 4's reputation on squishy ground indeed."

Many consumers do not draw fine distinctions. Writers of hard news stories and writers of editorials are both called journalists. Conventions of the news business, such as placing opinion pieces on special pages, are not enough to prevent confusion. Moreover, the news business contributes to the confusion when some journalists assume different hats at different times. So anything that makes it appear that there are no conspiracies behind the production of news is in the nation's best interest.

Leonard Downie Jr., the executive editor of the *Washington Post*, tells readers, "I no longer exercise my right to vote. As the final decision-maker on news coverage in *The Post*, I refuse to decide, even privately, which candidate would be the best president. . . . I want my mind to remain open to all sides and possibilities."

It is not necessary for journalists to give up a constitutional right if they are to continue to pursue a career in journalism. But etiquette requires that they should be sensitive to potential conflicts of interest, try to avoid them, and be forthcoming when there is a confluence of interest.

Public officials are restrained by conflict of interest laws or legally binding regulations. The etiquette for candidates defines conflict of interest as whatever they can't justify to their voters.

Consultants
(for Candidates)

IT WAS UNPRECEDENTED. He appeared on the cover of *Time* two weeks running. "THE MAN WHO HAS CLINTON'S EAR," September 2, 1996, profiles Dick Morris, "famous for casting a mighty and mysterious spell on the presidency." A week later "THE MORRIS MESS" is the tale of the consultant's resignation after a supermarket tabloid exposes his relations with a $200-an-hour call girl he allowed to listen in on a phone conversation with the president.

Another political consultant makes news in his own right when a front-page headline in the *Washington Post* proclaims, "ROLLINS: GOP CASH SUPPRESSED BLACK VOTE." According to the November 10, 1993, story, "Republican political consultant Edward J. Rollins said yesterday that the successful gubernatorial campaign of Christine Todd Whitman in New Jersey spent roughly $500,000 in 'walking around money' largely to suppress black voter turnout." The only trouble is Rollins's statement is untrue. His subsequent explanation: "Sometimes I have a weakness for grandstanding. . . . In the flush of victory, I spun out of control."

Memoirs follow notoriety. Morris clears $2.5 million on a book contract he secretly signed before being forced to leave the Clinton campaign. Rollins's book, also a best-seller, is deeply disloyal to those who

"Well, anyhow, our convention wasn't completely scripted"—copyright © 1996 by Herblock in the *Washington Post*.

pay for his services. California senatorial candidate Michael Huffington is "such a complete cipher he gave empty suits a bad name," wrote Rollins, who gladly took Huffington's money.

Rollins and Morris are not typical of the more than 3,000 people who engage in political consulting, many in such specialized work as designing polls, running focus groups, and buying TV time. The political consulting industry estimates it produced revenues of $10 billion in the 1993–96 election cycle. Campaigns are now big business.

But Morris and Rollins are increasingly typical of the credit takers. As entrepreneurs, consultants thrive as long as they attract clients—with tall tales as well as accomplishments. Candidates, some of whom are seeking office for the first time, may seek celebrity consultants almost as a talisman. ("I have Rollins therefore I am" might well have been the mindset of a Michael Huffington.)

"The tacit assumption of the political consultants," says historian Michael Beschloss, "is that the candidate is a lump of clay." Patrick Caddell, who no longer does campaign consulting, believes the fame of the consultant can give the impression of reducing candidates "to robots, to automatons." Hardly an inspiring impression for voters.

For the candidate, then, the etiquette should be that if your consultant is receiving more favorable attention than you are, fire the consultant. If your consultant is receiving negative attention, it goes without saying you fire the consultant.

Consultants
(for Journalists)

JOURNALISTS LOVE CONSULTANTS. Consultants understand the conventions of newsmaking. They are usually more available than candidates. They are good talkers. They speak the same language as the political press corps: strategies and tactics, polls and focus groups, TV buys and organizational support. Sometimes they are even the colorful rogues that reporters might have liked to be.

And they are necessary. Only a generation ago campaigns were run by political party operatives or by amateurs, friends and followers of the candidate. The decline of the parties and the rise of electronic technology has changed all that. Today's major campaigns need experts in audience response systems, split-sample polling, tracking polls, test-marketed advertising, audience and market segmentation, mall testing, cable TV purchases, and even something called "geographical information systems, which use digitalized maps to help produce geographical databases and visual renderings from demographic information."

There is no shortage of news about consultants, some very useful, particularly when a consultant crosses the line of acceptable behavior. Greg Stevens, working for Senator John Warner, doctors a photograph of his client's opponent for a TV ad. The story gets in the press and Warner fires Stevens.

The news media have the same obligations to cover consultants as they do others who influence public policy. Having helped elect legislators, do consultants then lobby them on behalf of corporate clients? This is a complaint made against consultant Frank Luntz, which he emphatically denies.

Even the private life of a consultant may be fair game if it significantly elucidates his political significance. According to *Boston* magazine, Republican consultant Arthur J. Finkelstein is gay yet designs strategies for outspoken opponents of gays. His client Jesse Helms ran an ad accusing "homosexuals" of "buying this election for [Democrat] Harvey Gantt" because Gantt "will support their demand for mandatory gay rights." Finkelstein's response: "I keep my private life separate from my business life."

When is a consultant filling a candidate's "empty suit"? Republican consultant Tony Fabrizio says, "I've had candidates ask me, 'What should my position be on abortion?' I tell them, 'if you don't know, you shouldn't be running for office.'" An amazing statistic from a 1996 survey of consultants: 44 percent agree that "when it comes to setting issue priorities, candidates are neither very involved nor very influential."

Although consultants are good stories, they tend to shift the focus of campaign coverage from the substance of issues to the politics of issues and veil what most matters: not who the consultants are, but who the candidates are; not what the consultants believe will work, but what the candidates believe.

The journalists' etiquette should be that the primary reason to cover consultants is to shed light on the people who wish to be our presidents, governors, senators, and other public officials.

Conventions

"THERE IS SOMETHING about a national convention that makes it as fascinating as a revival or a hanging," H. L. Mencken wrote of the Democrats' convention in 1924. "It is vulgar, it is ugly, it is stupid, it is tedious . . . and yet it is somehow charming. One sits through long sessions wishing heartily that all the delegates and alternates were dead and in hell—and then suddenly there comes a show so gaudy and hilarious, so melodramatic and obscene, so unimaginably exhilarating and preposterous that one lives a gorgeous year in an hour."

There are not many such moments anymore. The last time delegates arrived at a convention without knowing who they will end up nominating for president was 1952. Since then, with the exception of a few dramatic speeches and a "police riot" in Chicago in 1968, things have been pretty cut and dried. So one wonders what Ted Koppel had been expecting before he pulled out of the 1996 Republican convention because "nothing surprising has happened; nothing surprising is anticipated." Televising the conventions has turned them into TV shows, and TV networks have apparently now decided that TV shows are not worthy of coverage.

The broadcast networks (ABC, CBS, NBC) aired more than 100 hours in 1980. By 1996 coverage drops to less than 16 hours—one hour Mondays through Wednesdays, two hours on Thursdays when the nominees give their acceptance speeches. ABC cuts the last night of the GOP convention to 90 minutes: "just procedural stuff," says a spokeswoman. NBC runs an old episode of *Seinfeld* in place of vice presidential nominee Jack Kemp's speech. While those with cable TV have the option of viewing the conventions on C-SPAN or CNN or PBS, the vast majority of Americans either watch the gatherings on the networks or not at all.

The networks argue that their reduced schedules are only catering to weak consumer interest. Peter Jennings advises viewers, "If you haven't anything better to do, you might want to check in for an hour each night." Ultimately about 20 million people watch the 1996 conventions each night.

According to Dan Rather, "There's no real role for conventions." He calls the 1996 coverage the networks' last hurrah. The *Washington Post*'s Richard Harwood responds, "The 'average' viewer spends 832 hours a year watching commercially supported programs provided by the networks and their affiliated stations. Is four or eight or 10 hours every four years for a political convention a great burden for these prosperous enterprises?"

Even if the answer is obviously no, the case for convention coverage rests on the value of this public service. (TV and radio broadcasters have legal obligations to serve the public.) These massive gatherings of the two major political parties may not be surprising, but they are important. What journalists do with the opportunity is another matter. "If nothing else," writes Jim Naureckas, political conventions "provide a perfect news peg for taking a critical look at the platforms and public pronouncements of the major parties, explaining to citizens where they might take the country. What could be a more important function for journalists?"

The parties gather to present themselves in the best light possible; the challenge for the press is to explain what the parties offer the country. Will the networks further reduce coverage in 2000? Convention coverage is costly. The networks can correctly contend that the parties could do their business in three days—the four-day format is largely a way to help the convention cities earn back their financial commitments. Assuming

that the parties don't reform themselves to make conventions more central to the nomination of candidates, what might happen next is a nego-
tiation between the parties and the networks: cut back to three days in
return for a minimum two hours of nightly coverage.

The networks also need to reevaluate the form of convention coverage, which was invented by NBC in 1956 and has hardly changed in a
generation. As described by Bill Greener, the 1996 GOP convention
manager: "You get an hour and don't forget in that hour we have got to
get our commercials to air and our station breaks, and don't forget that
we need to showcase our talent, and don't forget that even before we
think about going to the podium we have to establish the presence of our
anchor and our four floor correspondents, and don't forget that after
that we are going to take a commercial break, and then we are going to
go back to the anchor, and then we might take what you've got going at
the podium."

Surely TV journalists can find interesting stories at the conventions.
"No matter how scripted they become," says CNN's Jonathan Karl,
"nowhere else are so many political sources assembled at one time."

Corrections

TUESDAY, FEBRUARY 27, 1996, is a particularly bad night for Ted Koppel, the anchor of ABC's *Nightline*. Perhaps the worst night in the history of that distinguished program. The program reports that Bob Dole has suffered "an embarrassing third-place finish in today's Arizona primary." Koppel ventures, "It is still far too early to be drafting a funeral oration for Bob Dole's presidential ambitions, but the candidate is not looking well, politically speaking." The report is incorrect: Dole has finished second. (Koppel later apologizes to Dole.) And the program concludes with Koppel apologizing "to all the Buchanans" for an earlier statement that Pat Buchanan's father "had been a regular listener to the radio broadcasts of Father Coughlin."

Media student D. Charles Whitney contends that "nothing is more crucial to a news organization than its reputation for accuracy and that nothing is more crucial to establishing this reputation than the honest, timely and public admission of errors." Yet, he notes, while consumers are most concerned with "subjective" errors—errors of analysis or emphasis, errors of a raised eyebrow or a harsh adjective—while news organizations are more concerned with factual errors, which they are more likely to correct. The two *Nightline* stories illustrate this distinction.

The profile of Buchanan on Friday, February 23, is complex and hard-hitting by TV standards. The broadcast's first segment focuses on the candidate's youth [Koppel voice-over]: "If there has always been an aura of certainty around Pat Buchanan, it was first nourished at home and here, at the Blessed Sacrament School. The Holy Cross nuns who ran the school conveyed the strongest sense of right and wrong and loyalty." A moment later, *Time* magazine's Lance Morrow, who was two years behind Buchanan in high school, opines, "The stability of that universe accounts for a lot of Buchanan's worldview today. I think he feels that that universe was betrayed, and there's a sense of something gone very much awry, and that it has to be set right by returning . . . to the universe of those certitudes."

"Buchanan's sense of certitude," Koppel narrates, "also derived from the other imposing force in his life, his father, Bill 'Pop' Buchanan, an arch-conservative, a supporter of Senator Joe McCarthy. Buchanan Senior also listened to the bigoted and isolationist radio orator Father Coughlin, who stirred populist passions and controversy on the eve of World War II." Koppel explains Coughlin's anti-Semitism. Morrow adds, "There was anti-Semitism to some extent among the students and I think that it was something of the traditional Catholic—well, the very bad tradition of the church, of the, almost of the 'They killed Christ' variety, the 2,000-year-old blood libel." *Nightline* reporters interview a Jewish neighbor who "remembers being called a Christ-killer and being beaten up by some of the younger Buchanan brothers. Not Pat," and another Jewish former neighbor says "that was never my experience."

In response, Bay Buchanan, the candidate's sister and campaign manager, attacks what she sees as the subjective error of Koppel's program, contending it is a "smear" against the Catholic Church to suggest that a Catholic school in Washington encouraged anti-Semitism in the 1940s and 1950s.

Nightline's retraction relates only to the narrow point of whether the senior Buchanan listened regularly to Father Coughlin. A fact. Other news organizations have reported this, says Koppel, "Still, we should have checked it out for ourselves. The Buchanan family insists the story is not true, and they, after all, should know. My apologies to all the Buchanans."

In the *Washington Post's* account of the Koppel-Buchanan exchange, the broadcaster defends his program as describing "the climate of the times" during the candidate's youth. "I sense that there is some confusion out there between being critical of Pat Buchanan and what is perceived as being critical of the church. There is not a line in there that is critical of the church as it exists today." As for Morrow's words, "To suggest the pre-Vatican II church was bigoted is not intended to offend anyone, it is simply a statement of historical fact."

Where Dole finishes in the Arizona primary is an easier call. *Nightline* is factually wrong. Thus journalists draw a line between factual and subjective error. The conventions of American journalism dictate that subjective error has to be addressed by other means—letters to the editor and op-ed columns in newspapers, making time available to aggrieved parties on TV.

Television's history of on-air corrections for even factual errors is discouraging. Bill Monroe recounts how NBC's *Today* show started an experimental letter to the editor segment in the early 1980s that the network correspondents detested and, "to keep his 'talent' happy," the producer eventually dropped. Emerson Stone, a former senior CBS News executive who writes an ethics column for *Communicator,* says, "When the occasional correction does appear, news volunteerism is a rare reason. In general the error was just too prominent to ignore in the community, a public commotion arose, or someone important complained." Structurally it is more difficult to work a correction into a TV program than into a newspaper. But Stone chides his former colleagues: "What, no creativity? Can't think of a way to make corrections interesting?" He argues, "Matters big enough to get into one newscast are big enough to be corrected in the next."

Newspapers have policies for correcting errors. Yet problems remain. According to *Washington Post* ombudsman Geneva Overholser, "Talk to *Post* reporters and you'll get an earful about how correcting is far from encouraged. If no one complains, don't raise it with your editors, they say they have learned; those editors don't want *their* bosses alerted that mistakes have been made. . . . And getting an editor to acknowledge that there really is a mistake can itself be a struggle."

A most sensible etiquette for corrections is formulated by the Organization of News Ombudsmen:

—Be aggressive in admitting mistakes and setting the record straight.

—Make it easy for consumers to point out potential errors.

—Assign one person to follow up on reports of errors.

—Make it easy for consumers to find corrections by running them in the same location.

—Develop constructive follow-up procedures for staff members who make errors.

Cyberpolitics

SOME FARSIGHTED journalists and scholars predict cyberspace "will have a profound impact on future elections" and may "even replace many of the representative structures that form the framework of our current constitutional system." But there is also the question of living with what one editor calls "electronic graffiti."

Without a crystal ball it is easier to look back to assess the functions that cyberspace, particularly the World Wide Web, is likely to perform in politics. Only about 4 percent of the voting-age population went on-line for information about the 1996 presidential election, but the uses were various:

—*The Internet as information pass-along.* The most useful political information on the Web in 1996 was simply the reconfiguration of media journalism. PoliticsNow, for example, was the electronic service of the *National Journal,* ABC News, *Washington Post, Los Angeles Times,* and *Newsweek.*

—*The Internet as information add-on.* A much smaller amount of reportage and commentary was created especially for the Internet, such as Microsoft's *Slate* magazine, generally with journalists recruited from the "old" media.

—*The Internet as propaganda.* This mainly consisted of the home pages of candidates and political parties, presentations ranging from the text of press releases to interactive components with dynamic graphics, sound, and music.

—*The Internet as organizational tool.* Campaigns also used the Internet for creating mailing lists, fund raising, volunteer recruitment, and a wide variety of intraorganization communications.

—*The Internet as conversation.* As an outlet for the opinions of Americans who are not often publicly engaged in political discourse, chat rooms were the Internet equivalent of talk radio. Indeed, talk radio hosts were well represented, with Michael Reagan's Web site even having a regular cartoon strip, "Adventures of Liberal Man."

The Internet, then, if 1996 is our guide, is performing functions that are otherwise performed in campaigns, only faster. Politicians and journalists are not creating new functions, nor are they likely to in the future, although the interactive sales pitch on the Internet when perfected will be a more creative vehicle than the current TV version.

There are, however, political consequences of an expanding Internet universe that will prove to be different from the early enthusiasm for cyberspace as a haven of participatory democracy. As political scientist Doris A. Graber notes, "In practice, cyberspace riches are available only to individuals with superior education and financial resources." So far the users of political web sites are more likely to be male, white, and wealthier than nonusers. Graber concludes, "The influence of educationally and economically privileged groups on politics, which has always been substantial, may be greatly enhanced."

Moreover, designing, maintaining, and updating Web sites can be a costly process. A study by Michael S. Margolis of the University of Cincinnati finds that major candidates and major parties in 1996 had far more elaborate Web sites than their poorer competitors. His conclusion: "Notwithstanding the novelty and explosive growth of electioneering in cyberspace, the Internet in general, and the WWW in particular, seem more likely to reinforce the existing structure of American politics than to change it."

The most immediate problem for consumers in cyberpolitics is to separate fact from fiction as we enter that brave new world where anyone with a computer and a modem can claim to be a journalist. Internet surfers can now discover that Princess Diana died as the result of a plot

hatched by the world's florists or that Vincent Foster was murdered by Mossad, the Israeli secret service.

Here's an appropriate etiquette for protecting yourself in cyberspace:

—Go back to square one wherever possible by reading the full text. What did the candidate really say? (The speech is on his Web site.) What's the party's position? (Find the party platform.)

—Ask questions. The wonder of the Internet is that the information giver is usually available.

—Develop a sense of smell. Does the information seem accurate (based on what you already know) and balanced? Are sources identified? Are they credible and authoritative?

—And if the information is important to you, always rely on multiple sources. (There are, for instance, more than 1,300 newspapers on-line.)

Debates
(Format)

TV DEBATES are now the central events of our presidential campaigns. Eighty-two million Americans watched the two debates in 1996. What their ground rules and formats should be, including which candidates to include and which to exclude, are therefore crucial to how we get the information we need to cast an informed ballot.

Let's first remind ourselves of the history of presidential debates and then return to the question of what we ought to do to improve them. There was no precedent in American history for general election debates when Richard Nixon and John Kennedy took seats in a Chicago television studio on September 26, 1960. (Lincoln and Douglas had debated in 1858, but they were running for the U.S. Senate; two years later, as candidates for president, they did not debate.)

Congress made the Kennedy-Nixon debates possible by suspending a requirement that would have forced the TV networks to give equal time to all the minor party candidates. Still, if debates are to take place, they require participants who expect to be able to gain from the experience. And usually one side has more to gain. In a contest between a backbench senator and a two-term vice president, the less well known Kennedy had the most to gain. Nixon's reasons for debating were probably more psychologically complex: he prided himself on his skill as a debater, and he may have underestimated his opponent.

The 1960 debates were watched or listened to by more people than had ever tuned in to a political event. The election was so close that a swing of less that 15,000 votes—properly distributed in a few states—would have reversed the outcome. Some conclude that Nixon's "unhappy appearance in the first debate" was the key to his narrow defeat. Future contenders would approach debates warily.

There were no debates in the next three elections. Lyndon Johnson was president in 1964, a time when some commentators argued that a president should not risk committing or embarrassing his nation through such overheated confrontations. The editorial voice of the *New Republic* asked, "Are a Chief Magistrate and the policies, the secrets, and the prestige of his regime to be made targets of direct, unrehearsed partisan interpellation—perhaps at a dangerous moment of world affairs?" In 1968 and 1972 Nixon, again the Republican nominee, was not about to repeat the error he believed had cost him an election.

If, in a sense, Nixon created the possibility of presidential debates by agreeing to meet Kennedy when it was not to his advantage, Gerald Ford could be said to have institutionalized debates by agreeing to participate in 1976 when he was the sitting president. And since his opponent, Jimmy Carter, won the election, Carter could hardly decline to debate when running for reelection in 1980. Nor could his challenger, Ronald Reagan, decline when he was president in 1984. By 1992 President George Bush reluctantly realized that candidates no longer have the luxury of avoiding debates. They are now tradition.

The debates in 1992 expanded to include independent candidate Ross Perot, a decision made by the bipartisan Commission on Presidential Debates composed of five Republicans and five Democrats, which had been set up in 1987 by the chairs of the Democratic and Republican National Committees.

Also in 1992 the commission changed the formats. After watching the 1960 and 1976 debates, Nelson Polsby pronounced, "In their present format presidential debates are uninteresting, uninformative, and unedifying." He was referring to the panel of journalists asking the

The Little Book of Campaign Etiquette

EACH MAN WILL BE ALLOWED A TWO-MINUTE CAMPAIGN RE-HASH

EACH MAY EMPLOY SOUND-BITES, GAFFE-TRAPS, RED HERRINGS, FLIP-FLOP BAITS, STATISTICAL OBFUSCATIONS, AND OUT-OF-CONTEXT QUOTES

JUDGING WILL BE SWIFT AND ARBITRARY

THANK YOU. I'D LIKE TO BEGIN WITH A COMBINATION WITTY-AND-SELF-DEPRECATING AGE-ISSUE DEFLECTION, PLUS A PITHY, BARBED, CHARACTER-TRASHING...

...AND I'LL RESPOND WITH A RESPECTFUL-YET-SUBTLY-CONDESCENDING, PAIN-FEELING, LIP-BITING, FAMILY-LADEN STATUS QUO APPEAL!

JOEL PETT

questions, which made the programs resemble joint press conferences, and the prescribed ninety-second or sixty-second answers, which resembled sound bites from the candidates' boilerplate speeches. The 1992 debates and those in 1996 added a single-moderator format and a town meeting format.

The commission excluded Perot in 1996, basing its decision on the advice of a distinguished panel of academics who concluded he did not have a "realistic chance" of winning the election. This was an unpopular decision. James A. Barnes wrote, "It will reinforce the suspicions of many voters that the two major political parties are corrupt partners in an arrogant Washington trying to protect their power from outsider challenges."

Returning to the central question of how we can improve a system that so importantly shapes the presidential contest, here are suggestions for consideration before the next election:

—Expand the membership of the Commission on Presidential Debates to include several persons not associated with the Democratic and Republican parties. The group choosing who's in and who's out should not be viewed as a self-protection society of the major parties.

—Create a two-tier system of debates: the first debate among presidential candidates who are on the ballot in all fifty states and the District of Columbia; all subsequent debates for candidates who have a realistic chance of winning. This provides incentive for party building, but recognizes that the debates primarily mean to help voters narrow their focus on those candidates who could be expected to carry the electoral college.

—Create a separate national televised debate for the presidential nominees of minor parties. This recognizes that these persons will not be elected, but reminds us that some important political ideas first came from minor parties.

—Continue to experiment with changes in format. As Alan Schroeder puts it, "Any programming strategy that advances the cause of voter education ought to be given a chance," such as holding some debates on a single topic or having the candidates question each other or holding debates built around hypothetical case studies (What would you do if . . .). Don Hewitt, the executive producer of *60 Minutes*, suggests a joint session of Congress during which the candidates debate for ninety minutes followed by "questions from both sides of the aisle, with Republicans throwing questions at the Democrats and Democrats grilling the Republicans." The year 2000, when an incumbent won't be running for reelection, could be a particularly good time to reevaluate the etiquette of debates.

Debates
(News Coverage)

THE NATIONAL PRESS CORPS has acquired some bad habits in recent elections. Reporting of the campaign debates is now (1) strategy oriented, focusing more on why candidates say what they say than on what they're saying, (2) filled with the worthless comments of the candidates' spin doctors, and (3) consumed with declaring winners and losers.

Compare today's stories with the accounts of the 1960 Kennedy-Nixon debates. Reports in the *New York Times* were a meticulous rendering of what the candidates said on the issues—with a rare aside such as, "The Vice President did not have the thin, emaciated appearance that worried Republicans across the nation during the first debate." The lead stories on the next debates, Ford-Carter in 1976, were in the same issue-oriented mode. In 1984, however, the emphasis changed notably, as illustrated by an October 8 story in the *Times*. Of the seven full paragraphs on the front page, this is how each began:

> *"President Reagan and Walter F. Mondale in blunt, sometimes highly personal exchanges . . ."*

> *"Mr. Mondale, who went into the debates trailing badly in the public opinion polls . . ."*

"The Democratic challenger turned in one of his most vigorous performances . . ."

"Some of the sharpest exchanges came over social issues . . ."

"For much of the debate, Mr. Reagan appeared less confident . . ."

"Reagan advisers also acknowledged that the President had been thrown on the defensive . . ."

"Moreover, it was unclear whether Mr. Mondale's performance would elevate his standing in the polls."

The new style of strategy/tactics reporting was the norm by 1992. The October 12 debate story in the *Times* said George Bush made "an effort to suggest that he understood the urgency of American economic problems, something many voters doubt." Ross Perot "may have gone some way toward regaining at least a bit of the credibility he lost when he abruptly walked away from the race in July." Bill Clinton "managed to tame his tendency to sound like a political-science professor." And this was the hard-news story. The *Times* also ran a front-page "assessment" story that began, "One way to score a presidential debate is to ask: What did each candidate need to achieve and did he do it?"

An emphasis on candidates' strategies reflects a press corps fascinated by matters of tactical thrust and parry and who must believe their consumers are equally fascinated. But there is no evidence to support this assumption. Certainly this focus is not as important to Americans as what the candidates are proposing to do about the concerns of the day. As such, debate reporting has become self-indulgent journalists' monologues attended to by like-minded members of an elite political community.

A hallmark of strategy reporting is that it is filled with the comments of campaign consultants and other political operatives. (Journalists quoted almost exclusively from the presidential candidates themselves in the debate coverage of 1960, 1976, and 1980.) The spin doctors arrived with the 1984 Reagan-Mondale debate, which offered the instant opinions of David Gergen, Bob Squirer, Tony Schwartz, Ed Rollins, Larry Speakes, and Lyn Nofziger. The trickle of spin-doctoring became a torrent by 1992, turning campaign workers James Carville, Mary Matalin, George Stephanopoulos, Paul Begala, and Stan Greenberg into celebrities. The debate logistics in 1996 included "Spin Alley" at the Hartford Civic Center where twenty pink laminated signs designated the persons the Clinton campaign had authorized to influence the media. "In some cases," according to the *Los Angeles Times,* "aides were trying to drum up interest, like barkers advertising their spinners." There is no reason to believe the spin doctors enrich our understanding of the issues.

The TV networks have concluded that the most important information they can impart is who "won." They arrive at winners and losers by conducting instant polls. CBS is most interested in this angle. ABC in 1980 aired a phone "poll" in which callers were charged 50 cents, an enterprise that ranks as one of television's more irresponsible moments. NBC in 1996 added an "insta-poll" in which viewers in a studio rated the debate by twisting dials. As politicians like to say—in this case correctly—the only poll that counts is on Election Day.

Reporters have a special explanatory obligation immediately after debates because so many charges and countercharges are flying about too fast to be properly absorbed by those who have not devoted their lives to parsing public policy. The news media can be most useful if it adopts a simple four-part etiquette:

—Focus on those portions of the debate that illustrate opposing views.

—Assess the accuracy and consistency of the arguments made by the debaters.

—Avoid the ancillary comments of partisan spin doctors.

—Avoid making instant polls the focus of debate coverage.

Disclosure

ON JANUARY 20, 1994, ABC's *PrimeTime Live,* with its hidden cameras, showed thirty congressional staffers on the beach in Key West, Florida, a trip paid for by a group of insurance organizations. The story's message, as pointed out by Alicia C. Shepard of *American Journalism Review,* "was that once again a trade organization was trying to buy votes on Capitol Hill." The year before, ABC's Sam Donaldson had spoken to the same group. He won't say what he was paid. He's a private citizen and doesn't write laws for the insurance industry, he says. A spokesman for the insurance industry says the journalist was paid $30,000 and has more influence on the public agenda than many members of Congress.

Jim Lehrer, who doesn't accept speaking gigs, says taking $30,000 from a group wouldn't influence his news judgments, "but if a member of Congress does that, we automatically assume that it's not only unethical, but the guy's on the take."

After asking ABC's Cokie Roberts about a 1995 speaking fee of $35,000 paid by a Toyota distributor, Shepard wrote, "Roberts doesn't want to talk about the company that paid her fee. She doesn't like to answer the kind of questions she asks politicians. She won't discuss what she's paid, whom she speaks to, why she does it or how it might affect journalism's credibility."

When John Harwood of the *Wall Street Journal* ran for a seat on the Standing Committee of Correspondents, the group that runs the congressional press galleries, his platform proposed that reporters should list their outside income, including speaking fees (sources, not amounts), on applications for credentials. He was defeated by his fellow correspondents.

Some news organizations prohibit their workers from making for-profit speeches. (That's their right as employers.) Some observers are upset that speakers get fat fees. (That's envy.) Some journalists contend that it's nobody's business since the news media are not government bodies. (That's a difference without a distinction when it comes to creating an above-board public society.)

The October 6, 1997, issue of *U.S. News & World Report* announced a new policy: it would regularly disclose the speaking engagements and fees of its staff members. "Bruce B. Auster: Marine Corps War College, $400; Amy Bernstein: Southern Methodist University, $2,000; Peter Cary: North Carolina State University, $500." And so forth. The editor commented, "The main surprise of this list may be . . . how modest the degree of such activity is. That revelation itself is a value of disclosure."

Nothing irritates politicians, especially members of Congress, more than the double standard they see journalists living by. (Members of Congress must disclose all sources of income annually and are prohibited from accepting honoraria.)

So how about *U.S. News*'s sensible etiquette? Every major news organization has its own Web site. A good place to post speaking fees. Start practicing disclosure.

Election Night

WHAT IS a proper etiquette on when TV networks should announce the outcome of presidential elections?

For voters living in the western half of the country this network practice has been a continual irritant. The networks declared Ronald Reagan the winner in 1984 at 8 p.m. EST. When they announced Bill Clinton's victory in 1996, according to a *New Yorker* writer, "Californians still had two hours left to boogie on down to the polling place and exercise their God-given franchise."

While the networks' predictions may be irritating, the more serious question is whether they discourage people from voting. In 1980 Jimmy Carter made an early concession speech, which Democratic politicians on the West Coast claim discouraged voter turnout and the loss of some local elections. Curtis Gans, director of the Committee for the Study of the American Electorate, believes declaring a winner produces a 0.5 percent to 3 percent drop in western state turnout. (Fifty-three statewide and federal elections in California, Oregon, and Washington were decided by 3 percentage points or less between 1980 and 1990.) But the question remains unsettled among professional observers. Warren

Mitofsky, the pioneer of Election Day exit polls, cites several studies that show no effect on voter turnout.

How accurate are the election night predictions? Ted Koppel says, "Perhaps there is a special little corner of hell reserved for journalists, where those of us from the electronic media will be forced to watch and listen to an endless loop of our inaccurate analyses and projections."

The key to election night predicting is a national exit poll conducted by Voter News Service (VNS), a partnership of the Associated Press and five TV networks, that surveys 60,000 voters as they leave polling places and conducts smaller surveys of statewide races.

New Hampshire polls closed at 7 p.m. in 1996. Six minutes before closing time VNS declared that U.S. Senator Robert Smith had been defeated by Congressman Dick Swett. But Smith won, 49.4 percent to 46.3 percent. Still, none of the networks reversed VNS's call until around 9:30 p.m.

Koppel and the rest of us long remember the bloopers. The networks' record in this regard, however, is very good. Between 1962 and 1992, for instance, CBS incorrectly declared winners in just 7 of 10,000 races. The exit polls—not perfect, obviously—remain an exceptionally valuable source of information for journalists and scholars.

Nor will the networks voluntarily drop the predictions that are such a valued part of their presentations. "To people in television," writes Tom Rosenstiel, "election night shows are the ultimate expression of the craft."

If the American people feel strongly that TV should not announce who wins the presidency until all polls are closed in the continental United States, the etiquette will have to be a congressional act mandating a uniform closing time for polling places from Maine to California, perhaps 10 p.m. in the east and 7 p.m. in the west.

Endorsements

THE RULE OF THUMB among newspaper people is that a paper's endorsement does not have much impact on a race for president. "I think there is an inverse ratio between visibility and influence," says Mindy Cameron, editorial page editor of the *Seattle Times.* "The more high profile an election, such as a presidential election, the less influence a newspaper endorsement has."

Fewer newspapers are making presidential endorsements. Thirteen percent were neutral in 1940; by 1996, 29 percent responding to a survey had a no-endorsement policy. *Editor & Publisher* magazine speculates that papers stop endorsing because many editors believe it doesn't make any difference. A *Chicago Sun-Times* editorial writer says, "Television has virtually replaced the newspaper editorial. People will go with their viscera."

But endorsements for president do have some impact—5 to 6 percent according to studies in 1964 and 1968—and endorsements on the senatorial and gubernatorial levels have clearer impact, particularly in getting readers to defect from their party's candidates.

Newspapers rarely disclose to their readers who is making the decision or what the endorsing process is. Sometimes the decisionmaker is obvious. When the *Union Leader* in Manchester, New Hampshire, the largest paper in the state, makes an endorsement (of Pat Buchanan in the state's 1996 presidential primary, for example), the choice is Nackey Loeb's—she owns the paper. But most papers belong to groups or chains, and the way they reach a decision is more veiled. At Scripps Howard Newspapers, for instance, all of the papers' editors gather to deliberate and vote for a candidate whom all papers then publicly

PETERS © Dayton Daily News & Tribune Media Services, Inc. Courtesy of Grimmy, Inc.

endorse. Chains with very large properties, such as Knight Ridder, whose papers include the *Philadelphia Inquirer* and the *Miami Herald,* usually make independent judgments at each paper.

Power may be variously arranged among editorial boards and publishers. The fifteen-member editorial board at the *Miami Herald* voted in 1984 by a margin of two-to-one to endorse Walter Mondale, but was overruled by the publisher and endorsed Ronald Reagan.

Readers will be pleased to know that when a team of scholars led by Professor Russell J. Dalton of the University of California, Irvine, conducted an elaborate research project on media coverage of the 1992 presidential election, they found no relationship between newspapers' formal endorsements and their news reporting of the campaign.

Etiquette demands that news organizations explain how they arrive at their endorsements.

(There is another type of endorsement. In 1992 Bill Clinton was endorsed by Barbara Streisand and Chevy Chase; George Bush by Frank Sinatra and Arnold Schwarzenegger; Ross Perot by Steve Martin and Sally Field. It is nice to know that these talented entertainers exercise their franchise. But must we also value their political opinions?)

Families

FOR A BRIEF moment in early 1996 it looked as if there might be a presidential contender's spouse who would remain a truly private person. Sabina Forbes, in a rare television interview, said, "I have never been involved in Steve's business decisions. . . . I have not been involved in decisions in the campaign, either." Her desire for anonymity may have been unrealistic, given the intrusiveness of the media. Was it also unreasonable, given the role she would have assumed if her husband had become the nation's chief executive?

Have the first spouses—historically still the first ladies—become too important to America to allow them space for privacy? Harvard ethicist Dennis Thompson describes "a principle of diminished privacy" in public life, meaning that the more power citizens give to officials, the less privacy the officials have a right to expect. To the president we award the most power, and to his wife, even though unelected, goes ceremonial and symbolic power. The position entitles its holder to be more than the nation's style setter. Even relatively traditional first ladies, such as Lady Bird Johnson and Pat Nixon, are reputed to have exercised behind-the-scenes influence. Rosalynn Carter attended cabinet meetings. Nancy Reagan affected scheduling and personnel decisions in important ways.

The unique public policy history of Hillary Clinton makes it even less likely that future spouses will be given the luxury of the media's inattention. Bill Clinton quipped in 1992 that he was running on a "Buy One, Get One Free" plan and once in office turned over to his wife the responsibility for developing a health care proposal that would be the most important item on his first-term agenda.

Her career in private law practice while her husband was governor also raises troubling questions. Newspaper columnist Marianne Means concludes, "Picking on the first lady, although mean, is within acceptable campaign bounds because she truly is the most influential president's wife in history, both in private and in public. With power comes accountability." (A professor of English has even written a disquisition on Mrs. Clinton's negative image in editorial cartoons.)

Perhaps male candidates—traditionally governors, legislators, vice presidents—are no different than they've always been. But their wives are. Elizabeth Dole, Adam Nagourney commented in the *New York Times,* "has more governmental experience than most of the candidates themselves." Among other 1996 contenders' spouses: Mrs. Phil Gramm, an economist, chaired the Commodity Futures Trading Commission; Mrs. Lamar Alexander was director of a child care business and former board member of the Corporation for Public Broadcasting; Mrs. Arlen Specter had been elected to the Philadelphia City Council. Their professional identities, however, do not exempt them from scrutiny if their careers are entwined politically and financially with those of their husbands.

Moreover, spouses are increasingly campaigners in their own right, surrogate candidates who travel with an entourage and have prime-time roles at the national conventions. The *Washington Post* described Elizabeth Dole in 1996 as "hurtling from city to city in a 14-seat corporate jet, the buttoned-up manager of a 30-person staff that includes an advance team of 12." (Even Sabina Forbes became slightly more visible after her husband lost in the Iowa caucuses and needed better publicity.)

When candidates are personally attacked, as political scientist Heather MacIvor points out, "spouses can be one solid clue to a candidate's character," as Hillary Clinton proved in her stand-by-your-man appearance on *60 Minutes* in 1992. Wives are also valuable assets when "family values" are a campaign's theme. In 1992 Marilyn Quayle, an attorney, appeared at more than 140 events during 40 days of campaigning.

MARGULIES © *The Record*. Reprinted with permission of Jimmy Margulies. All rights reserved.

In creating rules of etiquette for media treatment of spouses, journalists have the right to conclude that a spouse passes out of the "zone of invisibility" and is eligible for sustained attention when she

—has her own record of public activities, such as holding elective or appointive office,

—has connections to her husband of a political or financial nature, such as joint business holdings,

—does independent campaigning beyond the ribbon-cutting variety,

—makes herself a character witness in her husband's defense,

—or if she becomes an issue because of accusations leveled against her.

Since Sabina Forbes meets few of these criteria she deserves more privacy than other spouses of politicians. And there is even less excuse to write about Alma Powell if her husband Colin is not a candidate. But should either Mrs. Forbes or Mrs. Powell move into the White House, regardless of their reticence, they cannot remain in the zone of invisibility.

The spouse of a female candidate—possibly because of the novelty factor—will become even more visible than the wife of a male candidate if the press attention to the real estate deals of Geraldine Ferraro's husband John Zaccaro in 1984 is typical.

Children are another matter. Coverage of Chelsea Clinton illustrates that the mainstream press can be sensitive to a child's privacy when there is no overriding reason to be otherwise. Attention was modest and discreet through mid-1996. On her sixteenth birthday *Newsweek* ran a short article titled "A CHELSEA MORNING. RAISED IN FIERCE PRIVACY, SHE'S BECOMING A CHARMER." When a more public Chelsea emerged— first traveling to India and Bosnia with her mother, then appearing during her father's reelection campaign—the press was rightly attentive. But it was the Clintons who determined their daughter's involvement in matters that were clearly meant to be newsworthy. Hillary Clinton mentioned her daughter six times in the speech she gave to the Democratic National Convention.

There are cases of presidents' grown children who should expect ample coverage. Franklin Roosevelt, Ronald Reagan, and George Bush had children who were actively involved in their campaigns. Others earned notoriety because of actions of their own—one of Bush's sons was financially involved in a failed savings and loan—or who sought celebrity by writing books or becoming performers—as the Reagan children did—or for being in the company of those who are well known for their "well-knownness."

The media etiquette, given the principle of diminished privacy, is that there is rarely justification to enter the world of the children of presidents or potential presidents if

—they are young, meaning they still live at home,

—or they are not political confidantes of their parents,

—or they choose not to be celebrities,

   — or they avoid involvements that would be covered if they were not celebrities' children.

Focus Groups

NEWS STORIES based on the reactions of focus groups are now a staple of campaign reporting. The problem is that they almost always mislead us by implying projectability.

On the night of September 6, 1996, the *Washington Post* brought together ten uncommitted voters in Louisville, Kentucky, to watch the debate between the Democratic and Republican candidates for president. A front page article based on the gathering is headlined "FOCUS STILL FUZZY FOR UNALIGNED VOTERS." These ten voters apparently justify this attention because, as the reporter tells us, "about one in five voters say they only weakly support their choice or are undecided" and "these uncommitted voters are even more important in battleground states such as Kentucky." The implication, of course, is that ten undecided voters or ten soccer moms or ten angry white males represent all voters in such categories. They do not.

A focus group is a small number of people picked because of some common characteristic. They are usually paid for participating in a two-hour discussion led by a professional moderator, who is following a script. The findings of a focus group cannot be replicated. The group is not randomly selected and is not representative of any broader constituency. Indeed, pollster Mark Mellman comments, "There is no reason to believe that you have a group of average people in a focus group. Just think about the type of person who for forty dollars is willing to spend a couple of hours talking about things with a bunch of strangers."

Yet why did the *Post* focus on ten uncommitted Kentucky voters if we are not supposed to think (at least subliminally) that they are representative of all uncommitted voters? This is even suggested by mixing in scientific polling data ("one in five voters").

This is very different from an article based on a scientific poll in which some of the people who have been surveyed are quoted. The two types of articles will look very much alike, but the conclusion of "FOCUS STILL FUZZY"—"In the end, these uncommitted voters still remain loosely aligned"—is only a reporter's assessment of ten people in Louisville.

Readers and journalists need to understand that, as Warren Mitofsky puts it, "You cannot generalize from a focus group. There are no conclusions that come from focus groups that can be applied to a broader group of people." If editors can't restrain their enthusiasm for the pseudoscience of focus groups, etiquette dictates that they explain what this research technique does not do.

Free TV

CAN "FREE TV" put issues back into political campaigns?

In early March 1996 a group calling itself the Free TV for Straight Talk Coalition bought space in the *New York Times* to propose that the major networks provide between two and five minutes of prime time every weeknight during the final month of the presidential campaign for the candidates to talk directly to the voters on a topic of their choice.

The guiding spirits of this movement were Paul Taylor, a former *Washington Post* reporter, and Walter Cronkite, who said on *Nightline*, "I can't but believe that we would create a dialogue there that would so educate the American public that we would have an excited electorate going to the polls."

Ultimately the networks did make available various time segments, including four nights of two-and-a-half minute statements by the candidates on the *CBS Evening News*, five evenings of ninety-second statements on NBC's *Dateline*, and ten one-minute statements broadcast by Fox. A problem from the Cronkite-Taylor perspective is that the messages were not "roadblocked," TV jargon meaning broadcast on all networks at the same time. Also the free TV was aired during or adjacent to news programs, thus most likely seen by those already familiar with the candidates' positions, rather than the sitcom audience.

A more serious problem with the proposal had been predicted in March by Marvin Kalb: "There is no guarantee that [the presidential candidates] would take advantage of the time to present a more sub-

stantive explanation of their policy. . . . Indeed, since this free air time would be made available in the dwindling days and weeks of a long, exhausting campaign, it seems more likely that they would be cautious and use the extra time not for lofty discourses on public policy but rather for repeating time-tested slogans or tearing into an opponent's record."

That is exactly what happened. "It didn't work," concludes Dan Rather. Clinton and Dole "regurgitated sound bites they had been using since last summer. . . . What we got was a lot of waffling and sidestepping. The free time just took up time that otherwise would have been given over to good journalism." The *Chicago Sun-Times* gave free space as well and reports the same experience. "Much of what the candidates gave us was old material recycled word for word," writes the paper's editor, who calls the Clinton and Dole essays "a sorry charade."

"Listen, this was a first step," says Taylor. "These minispeeches were better than attack ads and sound bites." A study by the University of Pennsylvania's Annenberg Public Policy Center agrees that the candidates were more accurate and more positive in their free TV time than they had been on the same subjects in their commercials or the debates.

Given the length of presidential campaigns and the amount of news coverage devoted to the Democratic and Republican nominees, it is hard to imagine that attentive voters lack sufficient information to make a choice by Election Day. But this situation is only true of the race for president. Studies by the Rocky Mountain Media Watch illustrate the paucity of television coverage below the presidential level. Thirteen days before the 1996 election almost half of 68 local TV newscasts in 38 cities in 24 states contained no news of local, state, or municipal contests. It is on these levels that free TV opportunities for candidates can be of great value to voters.

One way to respond to this need is for Congress to create a "broadcast time bank" that Thomas E. Mann and Norman J. Ornstein have proposed. "It would provide free TV and radio time both to parties (to be allocated among their candidates) and directly to candidates who qualify for it (those who raise substantial funds in small, individual in-state contributions). The free time would be contingent on the candidates themselves delivering the messages."

Front Loading

CALIFORNIA POLITICIANS, preparing for the 1996 presidential campaign, move their state's traditional primary date from June to March. Frustrated by seeing nominations sewed up before their state's voters get a chance to cast a ballot, they also long for the attention the nation's media shower on Iowa and New Hampshire.

They are not alone. Legislators in Alaska, Louisiana, Delaware, and Arizona want the notoriety—and dollars—that come from being first. North Dakota and South Dakota see the beauty of having February primaries. (Twenty years ago Iowa and New Hampshire were the only February contests.)

Ultimately twenty-nine states choose to hold presidential primaries in March or before in 1996. Journalists dub the process *front loading,* meaning the nominees will be confirmed before California's rescheduled March 26 date.

In April 1996 a group of journalists and scholars come together to consider what has just happened. Rick Berke of the *New York Times* represents the journalists' consensus: "I think the short primary season cheated lots of voters and lots of journalists too out of a campaign.

I don't think enough people got a real opportunity to see the candidates except in three or four of the states."

Carl Leubsdorf, Washington bureau chief of the *Dallas Morning News*, adds that the candidates miss out as well by not campaigning in more states. "In past campaigns I've seen what candidates learned in all of these different places, and none of that happened this year." Curtis Gans

feels that "because the process is compressed, it forces candidates to raise $25 million in advance, both limiting the number of candidates who can meaningfully compete and making it possible for only those with substantial name recognition, personal wealth, or large Rolodexes to get into the fray." The historical record supports a longer campaign, says E. J. Dionne Jr.: "George McGovern's welfare plan [in 1972] didn't get debated until the California primary [in June]."

Other experts remain skeptical of an extended primary system. Maxine Isaacs contends, "We always assume that the public wants a long drawn-out process and benefits from it. There's not all that much evidence to support that." *Newsweek* columnist Meg Greenfield agrees: "So far as we voters are concerned," she wrote in February, "I don't think we could possibly stay tuned to this particular mud wrestle for more than the front-loaded-allotted month or so more."

Still, there are proposals for change. David S. Broder, the dean of America's political reporters, favors "a simple party rule saying that the convention would issue voting credentials only to delegates chosen on the first Tuesdays of March, April, May, and June of each election year. Any state could choose any of those four dates; the likely result would be a mixture of states from various regions on each of the four dates." *New York Times* columnist William Safire prefers clustering the states into "eight or ten regional primaries held during a span of about three months, preferably April through June." This has the added advantage of creating travel schedules that are cheaper and less exhausting for candidates and journalists.

Equally dissatisfied with front loading, the Republican party during its convention in San Diego adopts three changes in the rules under which it will conduct the next presidential nomination. It will try to prevent last-minute jockeying by states for an early primary date by requiring that a delegate-selection plan must be submitted by July 1, 1999. It will require primaries and caucuses to be held between the first Monday in February and the third Tuesday in June, which eliminates some January events. And it offers modest delegate bonuses to encourage states to come later in the process. These are sensible corrections. Surely we should be able to produce a more rational presidential campaign calendar.

Gender

Washington—Since Vice President Al Gore, often choking with sobs, told a disappointed crowd of supporters Monday that he has scrapped plans to seek the Democratic Party's presidential nomination, his display of emotion has raised questions about his fitness to be the nation's chief executive. "Is he tough enough?" "Could he negotiate with the Chinese?" "Could he pick up the red phone?" These are questions now being asked in political circles.

THIS NEWS of Mr. Gore is fiction. Yet it is based on real stories that were written about Congresswoman Patricia Schroeder when in 1987 she decided against running for president and cried while making her announcement. Would the press ask the same questions about the candidates' fitness if the crying politician were male? Perhaps. Perhaps not.

Some years ago business pages were full of a corporate controversy over whether William Agee, chairman of Bendix, showed favoritism in promoting his assistant, Mary Cunningham, to a senior level in the company. Ms. Cunningham's flaxen hair and green eyes figured prominently in the media accounts. Lacking were references to the color of Mr. Agee's hair or eyes.

Karen De Witt wrote an amusing article about the clothes of men candidates in 1995. "Senator Bob Dole is smartly put together, his suits dark, shirts white, ties conservative but not aggressively so." A New York–based magazine fashion editor says of Bill Clinton, "I wouldn't say he was well dressed." Thus a female journalist is having a little fun at the expense of male candidates, but female candidates invariably note the journalistic attention paid to their hairstyles, cosmetics, and clothing. *The Almanac of American Politics* notes the "charm" of U.S. Representative Nancy Pelosi and U.S. Senator Carol Moseley Braun without noting this quality in any of the male legislators; U.S. Senator Kay Bailey Hutchison, we are told, was "a prom queen," but we are not told that Senator Trent Lott was a cheerleader.

An etiquette for identifying a stereotype is to test it against the obverse.

Health

THE AMERICAN PEOPLE were not told they were electing a dying man.

Fifty years after the death of President Franklin D. Roosevelt, an article in the *New England Journal of Medicine* by Franz H. Messerli concludes, "it is obvious that over a period of only 10 years FDR had progressively severe hypertension that ultimately entered a malignant phase, leading to a fatal cerebral hemorrhage. . . . There is no doubt that FDR had quite severe and extensive arteriosclerotic disease." Yet the president's personal physician, Admiral Ross McIntire—an ear, nose, and throat specialist—claimed the president's health was excellent and the cerebral hemorrhage "came out of the clear sky," prompting Dr. Messerli to write that White House statements were either "a smoke screen or reflected the ignorance of some of the president's attending physicians."

More recent candidates' health records also contain examples of troubling information. John F. Kennedy suffered from Addison's disease, a treatable but incurable failure of the adrenal gland, which his family and physician denied during the 1960 campaign. Thomas Eagleton, Democratic nominee for vice president in 1972, was forced off the ticket when it was revealed he had electroshock treatments during hospitalizations for depression. Paul Tsongas, candidate for the Democratic presidential

*The Little
Book of
Campaign
Etiquette*

nomination in 1992, made an issue of his good health, including untrue statements by his doctors at the Dana-Farber Institute in Boston that he had not had a recurrence of cancer.

Indeed, candidates' health has been a matter of serious speculation in most of the elections since the Eagleton affair. The 1996 Republican nominee's elaborate release of health records was used to counter public concern about his age. A *Washington Post* article of July 21 begins, "On this Sunday before his 73rd birthday, Robert J. Dole plans, as usual, to spend 30 minutes on his treadmill." But according to the *New York Times,* Bill Clinton is "one of the least forthcoming of any presidential nominee in two decades about his health." Clinton's reluctance to release medical records prompted National Public Radio's Mara Liasson to ask at a White House briefing, "Does he have a sexually transmitted disease?" Liasson later explains, "It was the question hanging in the room." (The answer is no.) Media pressure subsequently results in Clinton's granting a half-hour interview to the *New York Times*'s medical reporter, which appears under the front-page headline "CLINTON, IN DETAILED INTERVIEW, CALLS HIS HEALTH 'VERY GOOD.'"

No information is more intimate than a person's medical records. Nor is the health of any one person more important to the nation than the president's. The case for full disclosure is made by Herbert L. Abrams, who believes that inherent in the act of running for president is giving up the right to medical privacy: "The public should be fully informed before they express their preference in the ballot; no claims of privacy, confidentiality, or privilege can obscure the obligations of the candidates to be candid with the electorate."

George J. Annas, however, stresses that a candidate's privacy in most cases outweighs the public's right to know. "Unless we want to discourage our presidents, presidential candidates, and possible presidential candidates from seeking medical assistance in times of physical and psychological distress, we must show at least some respect for their medical privacy by setting limits to expected disclosures."

An excellent etiquette, developed by political scientist Robert S. Robins and psychiatrist Jerrold M. Post, would be partial disclosure in the form of a written report from the candidate's physician with refer-

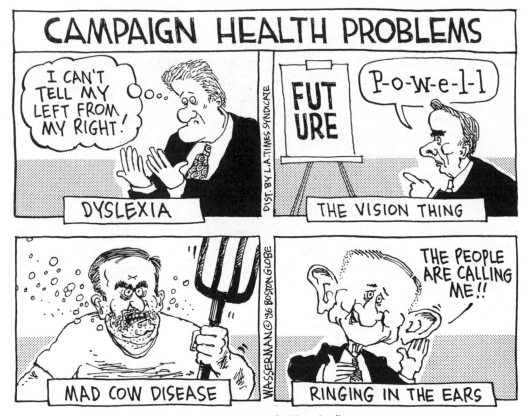

WASSERMAN © *The Boston Globe.* Distributed by the Los Angeles Times Syndicate.

ence to specific health problems and their treatment, an approach that is analogous to screening for other professional jobs.

Robins and Post make four sensible assumptions on which to base an assessment of what we need to know in order to choose a healthy president: "(1) Presidents need not be perfectly healthy to function effectively in the oval office. . . . (2) The public is as capable of evaluating medical information, including the disputes that may develop between groups of medical experts, as of any other type of scientific material. . . . (3) The more fully the public is informed . . . the better the quality of the public decisionmaking. . . . (4) Privacy rights are conditional upon the nature of the occupation."

Candidates' health and wealth are the two subjects about which journalists have a special obligation to be nosey. Both subjects could yield information that might be disqualifying. Still, we must keep in mind that of the ten most recently elected presidents—Roosevelt through Clinton—only Roosevelt died in office of a disease that could have been made known to voters.

America, moreover, has inadvertently created the most arduous leadership selection system in the world. Our obstacle course of primaries and caucuses is roundly faulted for many reasons. It is certainly obscenely expensive. It rarely promotes reasoned debate. It obviously turns off many eligible voters. It does not test for many of the qualities necessary for a candidate to be an effective president. But as a stress test, it is hard to imagine a better gauge of a future president's physical stamina.

Horse Race

WHO'S AHEAD? The longest-standing criticism of how the press covers presidential campaigns, particularly when candidates for the Democratic and Republican nominations are contesting state primaries, is that the reporting is overwhelmingly about the "horse race."

Who cares? Not the voters. According to a 1996 Roper survey, only 22 percent are very interested in these stories; 46 percent believe the media are too focused on winning and losing.

Yet horse-race coverage keeps increasing. It doubled in the *New York Times* from 1948 to 1992. And there was more attention to the horse race in 1996 than in 1992, according to Robert Lichter and Ted Smith, even though Bill Clinton was unopposed for his party's nomination. "Fully 47 percent of all 1996 primary stories included extensive discussion of a candidate's election prospects, up from 37 percent four years earlier." When they broaden the definition of horse race to include coverage of campaign strategy and tactics, the number of stories almost doubles—from 181 in 1992 to 269 in 1996. The TV networks ran more than 1,500 horse-race stories by the end of September. Typically, as reported by Jeff Greenfield on ABC on September 15, "all the stories are about how far behind Dole is. The stories may be wrong . . . but it's hard to get people juiced up about an election that doesn't look close."

To charges that the press corps overemphasizes the horse-race aspects of campaigns, veteran Associated Press writer Walter Mears responds that this "is not a vice because a presidential campaign is a horse race." Press critic Robert Manoff agrees: "If we want to see another kind of reporting, we are first, as a people, going to have to create another kind of politics."

BENSON © *Arizona Republic.* Reprinted with permission of Steve Benson and United Media Syndicate. All rights reserved.

Perhaps. But it's also true that horse-race stories (a) are easy to write, (b) can't be proved wrong at the time they are written, and (c) fascinate political reporters, if not Main Street consumers.

After examining the pros and cons of horse-race coverage, political scientist Graham P. Ramsden concludes, "Clearly, while the horse race needs to be covered, it deserves much less coverage than it has been getting." A cautionary etiquette then is that each time reporters sit down to write a horse-race story they should consider that the news hole is finite. Space devoted to the horse race is space not devoted to something else (the finer points of a candidate's tax proposal? a candidate's experience as an executive?). And, of course, we will ultimately find out who wins the horse race without any help from them.

Labels

"IMAGINE, for a moment a political discussion without the words 'left,' 'right' or 'conservative,'" writes E. J. Dionne Jr. "CNN would have to take *Crossfire* off the air. Rush Limbaugh would go back to being a disk jockey again and John McLaughlin might rejoin the priesthood. . . . If we would not be lost without those words, we would certainly be rhetorically and conceptually challenged."

We may be even more conceptually challenged because of such words.

The trouble with labels is especially apparent every fourth year when journalists try to sort out the candidates seeking the presidency. When researchers counted the most frequently used media terms to describe the 1992 presidential contenders, they discovered that 40 percent of the characterizations referred to "liberal," "conservative," or "moderate."

Television networks are severely criticized for their use of labels by L. Brent Bozell III, who is less concerned about the practice of labeling than about media bias—conservatives, he contends, are more likely to be insidiously labeled as extremists. Yet Newt Gingrich's former press secretary Tony Blankley did a computer search linking "liberal" and "Hillary" and got 2,485 hits. Labeling is a game that both "left" and "right" can play.

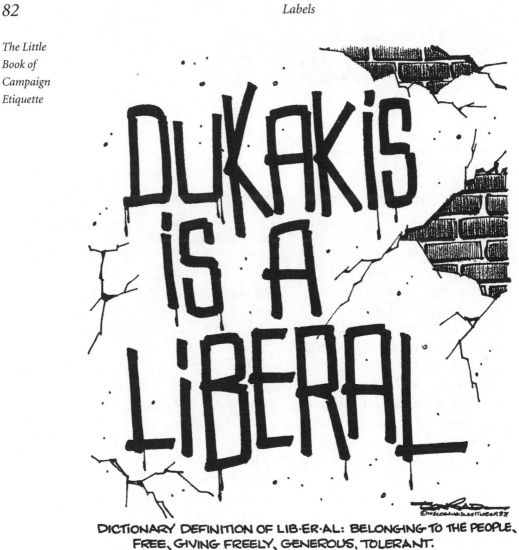

DICTIONARY DEFINITION OF LIB·ER·AL: BELONGING TO THE PEOPLE, FREE, GIVING FREELY, GENEROUS, TOLERANT.

CONRAD © *The Los Angeles Times*. Distributed by the Los Angeles Times Syndicate.

No political player is as befuddling to the labelists as Pat Buchanan. A Pew Research Center poll lists the public's single-word descriptions of him as "extreme," "radical," "conservative," and "ultraconservative" (in frequency-of-use order). What is he? A cultural conservative? Assuredly. An economic conservative? No. A populist? Maybe. An isolationist? Mostly. The media's attempts to label him prove unhelpful.

Simplistic and misleading ideological scales are not standard operating procedure in all types of national reporting. U.S. senators are most often identified by their position (such as "a member of the Intelligence Committee"), followed by a stand on an issue ("pro-abortion"), a specialty ("an expert on military affairs"), a personal characteristic ("tall" or "short"), and only then by ideology.

Variations on liberal-moderate-conservative fit comfortably into presidential campaign reporting because of the media's focus on the horse race. If the contest is a horse race, it becomes convenient to give each jockey an ideological position on the track. Richard Harwood writes of his fellow journalists, "Often we fling labels around as a sort of emotional impulse, having only the fuzziest notions of what they mean or what we are trying to convey to the audience." Communications experts Doris Graber and David Weaver would like journalists to "revise the focus of coverage to provide more relevant information for making informed choices." In the meantime, journalists should do no harm. When in doubt, avoid ideological labels.

Local TV News

IF YOU WERE WATCHING KCBS's 11 p.m. news in Los Angeles on March 24, 1997, you saw a skateboarding dog. Four days later you saw Easter egg–hunting chimpanzees. What you did not see, according to a study conducted at Cal State Northridge, is any news about the election for mayor of Los Angeles, scheduled for April 7. Two weeks before the election there are no stories on KCBS or KNBC. On election day minus three KNBC finally airs a campaign story of singer Sheryl Crow performing at Sean Penn's nightclub for candidate Tom Hayden's fund-raiser. Ultimately the two stations combined show 5 minutes 25 seconds of political news in 15 days. (During the same period viewers can see 22 minutes 45 seconds of political advertising.)

Los Angeles stations are below average in the percentage of stories they devote to government and politics (4.5 percent). A survey of thirteen cities drawn from the top twenty-three markets shows that during October 1996, the month before the presidential election, 7 percent of the stories in the most popular local news programs are about candidates. Crime stories account for 22 percent of the total.

Local TV news programs are the most popular and trusted source of information in the United States. The Pew Research Center finds 65 percent of all adults say they regularly watch local news, and 42 percent watch network news. In a Harris poll 57 percent of those surveyed name local TV news as either their most important or second most important news source, with network TV at 39 percent, newspapers 33 percent, and radio 16 percent.

And there is a growing menu of local TV news programming. Where once it was the half-hour before we turned in for the night, increasingly we are surrounded, often from 5:00 to 8:00 in the morning, and for an hour or ninety minutes at suppertime.

The success of local TV news—other than its prurient appeal ("Rapist trapped on Main Street. Film at 11!")—is its immediacy to viewers' lives, an amalgam of weather, sports, and community events. Yet what is so stunning about local TV coverage of the 1996 elections is how much more attention is paid to national elections than to local ones.

A volunteer organization in Denver called Rocky Mountain Media Watch taped the evening local news on three Wednesdays—eight weeks, five weeks, and two weeks before the 1996 elections—tuning into 90 stations in 46 cities. The results:

—*Eight weeks before election.* Seventy percent of stories focus on the presidential contest, 27 percent of stations have no election news, and 73 percent broadcast no local, state, or municipal election news.

—*Five weeks before election.* Fifty-seven percent of stories are about the presidential race and 69 percent of the stories in 43 cities have no news of state, municipal, or local contests.

—*Thirteen days before election.* Sixty-two percent of stories are on the presidential race and 45 percent of local newscasts have no stories about local, state, or municipal contests.

The etiquette for local TV news directors in stations that are supposed to be the voice of their communities is to ask, "If we are not reporting local elections, who will?" Then act accordingly.

Lying
(for Journalists)

❧✦❧

"JOURNALISTS, who are in the business of telling the truth, should not lie," says Marvin Kalb, former correspondent for CBS and NBC, now Harvard's Edward R. Murrow Professor of Press and Public Policy. Why is a proposition so simple so controversial in journalism circles?

The "right to lie" has been heatedly debated in recent years because of two TV newsmagazine stories aired in 1992. NBC's *Dateline* was caught in multiple lies when it created a flaming crash to try to prove that GM trucks with the gasoline tank mounted outside the frame are unsafe. ABC's *PrimeTime Live* lied when its producers faked employment records and job references while trying to expose Food Lion supermarkets for allegedly selling tainted meats.

Exposing unsafe vehicles and unhealthy food is good. Lying is bad. What's a journalist to do? According to the Society of Professional Journalists' handbook on ethics, as summarized by Susan Paterno, lying or deception may be used only when all other means have been exhausted, when the story illustrates an extremely serious social problem or prevents profound harm to individuals, when the journalists reveal their deception to the public, and when the harm prevented by the information outweighs the damage caused by the deception.

But even these sensible guidelines fudge a very important point: Journalists' deceptions are often illegal.

There is no First Amendment immunity from ordinary rules of criminal law or from tort rules that are not aimed at speech. As James Boylan, the founding editor of the *Columbia Journalism Review,* notes, "Many journalists mistakenly assume that the First Amendment protects reporters wherever they choose to go, whatever they may do in the pursuit of a story." The Constitution protects media content, not media newsgathering. "In other words," says Joan Konner, "journalists are not above the law."

Too often, however, as in the Food Lion deception, when journalists get caught they respond that the law shouldn't apply to them because they are good people with good reasons to lie.

While breaking the law is associated mainly with investigative journalism, not political reporting, I do recall the story of one overzealous reporter who "gained entry by subterfuge" into a California congressman's office in order to get a story on his reelection plans.

Journalists' etiquette should be that if they insist on breaking the law, in or out of covering campaigns, they must also be willing to pay the price. This is the concept of civil disobedience used effectively by civil rights advocates in the 1960s. Otherwise, journalists' excuses for lying are no better than politicians' excuses.

Lying
(for Politicians)

POLITICIANS TELL four types of lies: honest lies, inadvertent lies, half-truths, and damn lies.

The honest lie happens when a politician is president and the president's press secretary or other spokesperson has information that could endanger lives and national security. Jody Powell, President Carter's press secretary, wants to protect the mission to rescue Americans held hostage in Iran. The Reagan White House wants to protect U.S. troops invading Grenada. In both cases they engage in honest lying.

Inadvertent lying happens because, as Bill Moyers recalls from his days as President Johnson's press secretary, "At times circumstances make a liar out of you." There is always the possibility that information given out today will turn out to be wrong tomorrow. According to a former Pentagon spokesman, "Half of the initial internal reporting within government in a crisis is wrong."

Half-truths are an effort to tread the line between truth and falsehood, often by narrowly defining a reporter's question. President Clinton's press secretary, Michael McCurry, calls this "the art of telling the truth slowly." Here is an example from a State Department briefing:

Q. Has the assistant secretary of state been invited to China?

A. No. (Meaning: *He will go to China as an adviser to the vice president. It is the vice president who will be invited. Therefore, the*

Reprinted with permission of Stephen Templeton. All rights reserved.

spokesman is not lying. Rationale: *The spokesman feels he must say this because protocol requires that the Chinese must first publicly extend the invitation.*)

A damn lie is Senator Joseph McCarthy telling a West Virginia audience in 1950: "I have here in my hand a list of 205 [communists] who were known to the secretary of state and who nevertheless are still working and shaping the policy of the State Department." McCarthy had no list. Damn lies are not necessarily big lies. The Nixon White House lied when it announced that Tricia's wedding cake was an old family recipe. Anthony Marro later concluded, "A White House that would put out misinformation about the origins of a cake recipe probably couldn't be expected to tell the truth about the war in Cambodia."

Reporters tend to accept honest lying, understand inadvertent lying, fail to work hard enough at exposing half-truths, and gleefully go after damn lies.

Lying is a complicated and fascinating subject, as Sissela Bok's 350-page book on it illustrates. And politicians may be better at it than most of us. At least that is a possible conclusion from a study by Colgate University psychologists who discovered that the best liars among preschoolers are also the leaders during play period.

Most of us understand when Al Gore or Dick Gephardt says in 1998 that he is not running for president that they're lying. But we're not harmed by this blather. Since lying is expressly forbidden in the Ten Commandments, it may be sacrilegious to propose yet another rule for politicians, but this etiquette would improve civic dialogue and help restore trust in government, so here goes: Thou shalt not say anything deceitful that could appear on the front page of your hometown newspaper.

Metaphors

A PRESIDENTIAL CAMPAIGN is supposed to be something special—the Super Bowl of the news business," we are reminded by the *Washington Post*'s Richard Harwood. For journalists it is a time to roll out Big Metaphors, colorful words or phrases that help us better understand what is going on by suggesting comparisons with things that we already understand.

The most often used metaphors are drawn from sports, as Harwood's metaphor suggests. Sometimes they are unusually creative, as when Albert Hunt of the *Wall Street Journal* advises Bob Dole "to abandon his conventional half-court offense and adopt a higher-risk, pressing, trapping transitional game," or when Sam Fulwood of the *Los Angeles Times* views Dole as "a proud champion boxer, stunned momentarily by a lesser contender's lucky punch yet still cocky enough to believe he will eventually win the fight." More often the metaphors are very tired clichés. Steve Forbes "takes off the gloves" or Lamar Alexander is "on the ropes."

Coverage of Republicans in 1996 saw a rise in the religious metaphor, reflecting perhaps the influence of the Christian Coalition. This is especially true of the way the press reports on Pat Buchanan,

CUPID

who demonstrates "his ability to generate a religious fervor for his campaign-cum-crusade" (*Christian Science Monitor*), who is "apocalyptic" (*U.S. News & World Report*), a "preacher" whose supporters "worship a lost 'Ozzie and Harriet' America" (*Newsweek*).

More disturbing campaign images are of warfare. Bold *Newsweek* headlines in 1996 proclaim "THE GROUND WAR" and "THE PHONY WAR," although the stories underneath describe nothing more chilling than a bunch of politicians vying for a nomination. Reporters are fond of *battleground* and *battlefield, skirmishes* and *war chest.*

There is evidence to suggest that use of the campaigning-as-warfare metaphor has increased with the rise of the consultant in American politics: opposition research, a fast-growing specialty of the consultancy industry, resembles military intelligence; espionage is reminiscent of tactics now associated with Watergate; war propaganda is very much like the patriotic symbolism that was featured in Lee Atwater's advertising for George Bush in 1988; and James Carville's rapid response campaign for Bill Clinton in 1992 came from his now famous "War Room."

Do bellicose metaphors have consequences?

As a political etiquette, journalists should consider these words of Nebraska Public Radio's Carolyn Johnsen: "If Americans view the democratic process simply as a matter of vanquishing the foe and taking territory, there is less probability that policymakers will choose the alternatives of constructive debate, compromise and collaboration."

Money

ADDRESSING POLITICAL CANDIDATES in general, University of Massachusetts professor Ralph Whitehead says, "How much money you have and how you got it falls right across the question of whether I as a voter can trust you with my car keys."

There has been a great deal more openness about money in recent years. It would be difficult to imagine Lyndon Johnson or John Kennedy making public the sort of personal financial information that now comes almost routinely from presidential contenders.

When Geraldine Ferraro made public her tax returns in 1984 the *New Republic,* tongue in cheek, questioned "whether anyone inept enough to pay 40 percent of her income in taxes is qualified to be Vice President of the United States." When he was governor of California in 1970, Ronald Reagan legally paid no state income tax.

Candidates for president are now required to file a financial disclosure statement (as are members of Congress). Because the forms list assets, income, and liabilities in broad ranges rather than precise amounts, they only hint at candidates' actual worth. For example, the top category is "over $1,000,000," and in 1992 Ross Perot listed 176 separate holdings in that category.

Many candidates are also voluntarily releasing their federal income tax returns. Bob Dole in 1996 may have set a record by putting out three decades of tax information. In addition, Dole asked for an assessment by the accounting firm of Price Waterhouse, which declared the taxes paid to be "materially correct." President Clinton made public his returns dating back to 1977. Pat Buchanan's portfolio showed he owned stock in many companies he was attacking for laying off workers. Lamar Alexander provided extraordinary access to his business ventures, for which he paid a political price when Steve Forbes attacked one of his deals in a radio ad.

Forbes, on the other hand, refused to release any personal financial information beyond what was required by the Federal Election Commission. He said that calls for his tax returns were "simply a diversion." Others saw the information as especially relevant in that the centerpiece of his campaign was the proposal for a 17 percent flat tax that would eliminate taxes on unearned income.

Media etiquette about candidates' wealth—how they make a living, their assets and liabilities, the taxes they pay—is best stated in a 1988 *Washington Post* editorial: "Particularly in the case of candidates for president, voters have a right to examine and cross-examine, backward, forward and upside down."

News Councils

WHO WATCHES the watchdog?

Journalists keep a steely eye on politicians and others in public life. It is a fearsome responsibility. And when they get it right, there is no task for which we honor them more. Yet they don't always get it right. What then are our options?

—Appeal to the offending news organization: write a letter to the editor; ask for a correction; call the ombudsman, if there is one.

—Appeal to the courts: sue for libel; seek an injunction.

—Appeal to the marketplace: organize a boycott; cancel your subscription; turn to another channel; withdraw advertising.

But even journalists agree that these alternatives are not very satisfactory.

From 1973 to 1984 there was also something called the National News Council, a nongovernmental group of journalists and private citizens who judged complaints and issued reports on the fairness of individual stories. Even though it ruled against the media in only 82 of 242 cases, the editor of the *Boston Globe* complained, "They have no damn business meddling in our business." Ultimately the council died because major media companies, notably the *New York Times* and *Washington Post,* refused to cooperate.

*The Little
Book of
Campaign
Etiquette*

In Minnesota, however, there has been a successful news council in operation since 1970. It works because the state's news organizations want it to work. The council consists of twelve journalists and twelve members of the public, presided over by a nonvoting justice of the Minnesota Supreme Court. While some members have important affiliations, such as president of the Federation of Teachers or executive director of the Better Business Bureau, "they must check that representation at the door" and vote as individuals.

The rules are simple. (1) Only those who are the subject of a story can file a complaint. (2) Complainants must agree to waive the right to sue. (3) Complainants speak for themselves; no lawyers are involved. (4) Complaints must relate to information that has been printed or aired. "What a news medium has actually done, not what it has not done" is at issue, says Bob Shaw, the council's first director.

The Minnesota experience was largely unnoticed outside the state until Mike Wallace brought a *60 Minutes* crew to observe a complaint by Northwest Airlines against WCCO-TV in October 1996. After a three-hour hearing the council voted nineteen to two that the two-part series on the company's safety record and maintenance practices was "distorted, untruthful." The verdict stunned the program's anchor, Don Shelby. "This is a dishonor to me," he told the council. But three months later a recovered Shelby gave a thoughtful interview on what was wrong with the story.

Mike Wallace's story has turned him into an advocate for reviving the news council concept. At first he wanted to revive a national council, but he later concluded that this format would be unwieldy and that state and city news councils would be more workable. Yet news councils are still vigorously opposed by such media giants as Don Hewitt, executive producer of *60 Minutes*, and Joseph Lelyveld, executive editor of the *New York Times*. They usually make three arguments:

First, says Lelyveld, "We have a deep concern that voluntary regulation can lead, bit by bit, to more serious kinds of regulation."

Second, journalism should not be judged by nonjournalists. Hewitt says, "Are journalists as good as they think they are at avoiding bias? No, nobody is. But at least journalists are trained to report fairly—unlike corporate executives, academics, PR types, and assorted members of the citizenry who have the time and the inclination to sit on a news council."

Third, criticism by a news council might discourage the sort of hard-hitting stories that are most needed and are most apt to draw complaints.

The prospect that the existence of a news council would lead to regulation should be taken seriously. But critics never explain what regulation and how a news council could lead there. Instead, the argument is always left dangling. Given First Amendment protection and that a news council's nonlegal decisions are not precedent in a court of law, this is no more than a undefined worry.

Argument number two—no one is qualified to watch the watchdog—is ludicrous. It is hard to be a good journalist, but the fundamental principles of good journalism are few and easily understood.

As for argument three—the "chilling effect" of news council criticism—Wallace counters that removing the prospects of libel suits could actually embolden news organizations.

Wallace is right. Consumer skepticism about the media makes the news council concept much more important today than it has ever been.

The only power a news council has is the power to embarrass. This is a potent power in a society of professionals. But it is not too high a price to pay to ensure a healthier and more respected journalism.

Platforms

※◆※

PARTY PLATFORMS are often dismissed as, in the words of Wendell Willkie, "fusions of ambiguity" and as being "all but forgotten as soon as the last balloon is swept from the convention floor." Both criticisms are provably wrong. Indeed, as Rutgers professor Gerald Pomper observes, if the platforms are so meaningless, what are the delegates fighting so fiercely about?

Platform drafters engage in collective bargaining over where their parties should stand on the major issues of the day. Some of the results of this labor are mere bombast, of course, and some amount to nothing more than pointing with pride (for the in-party) or viewing with alarm (for the outs). "*We do pledge a government that has as its guiding concern the needs and aspirations of all the people*" (from the 1976 Democratic platform). But half of all platforms consist of policy proposals, often in remarkably precise language. On abortion, for instance, Democratic platforms are "pro-choice" and Republican platforms are "pro-life." Those who accuse Republicans and Democrats of being Tweedle dum and Tweedle dee do not bother to compare the planks in their platforms.

At least four studies have compared platform promises and the subsequent actions of presidents, each study spanning a minimum of seven presidencies. All reach the same conclusion. Presidents prefer to keep their word, if only because it's when they don't that they get in trouble. (Remember George Bush's "Read my lips . . . no new taxes"?)

Presidents honor nearly two-thirds of their promises and ignore only a tenth, according to one study. Another, published in 1985 by Professor Jeff Fishel of American University, concludes, "Every president, from Kennedy through Reagan, has demonstrated considerable good faith, seeking through legislation or executive order to follow through on a majority of his campaign pledges."

Recommended etiquette for journalists and voters: take platforms seriously; the candidates do.

HANDELSMAN © *The New Orleans Times-Picayune*. Reprinted with permission of Walt Handelsman. All rights reserved.

Polls
(for Journalists)

ONCE EVERY fourth year, radio station KEMB in Emmetsburg, Iowa, asks listeners to flush their toilets when they hear the name of their favorite candidate for president. Thomas E. Mann and Gary R. Orren explain why: the station "can then measure the support for each candidate because the water level at the local sewage treatment plant declines 1 inch for every 135 flushes. The station is proud of the forecasting accuracy of its poll, but concedes that there is some inadvertent voting." Most media polls are more elaborate.

Media polling is a growth industry. In 1972 news outlets commissioned 2 presidential election polls; in 1996 more than 800 national polls. Besides the TV networks, media pollsters now include more than half of all local TV stations and almost all the large-circulation newspapers. "The truth is," says CNN's Jeff Greenfield, "we have gone absolutely out of our minds about polls."

This polling miasma leaves in its wake a lot of confused consumers. Half of all Americans do not believe the election polls, according to an ABC poll. How can it be that in June one poll gives Bill Clinton a sinking lead of 15 percentage points over Bob Dole and another poll gives him a rising lead that is only 6 points ahead? Why does the final CBS poll claim Clinton has 53 percent and Dole 35 percent when the actual election result will be 49–41? Pollsters have a lot of explaining to do.

Knowledge about polling is important not only because polls influence voters, but because they also influence journalists and what they report.

How is a survey question worded? Edwin Diamond and Robert A. Silverman tell of a telephone survey asking if the government is spending too much money "on assistance to the poor." Twenty-three percent of respondents answer "yes." Then a question asks if the government is spending too much money "on welfare." Now 53 percent respond "yes."

When is a survey taken? Pollsters find that people are least likely to be home or least willing to answer questions on the weekends. Saturday is a particularly risky day to find a representative cross-section. (Weekend respondents are apt to be older and more liberal.) There are also differences that relate to the time of day.

How hard is a pollster trying? What is the policy for calling a potential respondent a second time if he or she is not reached the first time? People are getting harder and harder to poll. Americans are increasingly hiding behind their answering machines, don't answer the phone, or simply refuse to answer the questions. In 1992 the level of nonresponse in exit polls averaged 42 percent.

Who is doing the polling? Charles E. Cook says polls done by colleges are "sometimes conducted by marketing professors with little knowledge of politics or political science professors who, in many cases, have little practical experience. Additionally, many of these university-sponsored polls are conducted by students, sometimes with little supervision."

Will a poll respondent actually vote? Different polling organizations have different ways to make this judgment.

News organizations that commission polls may not tell us the results of rival polls. Yet as Michael R. Kagay explains, "In polling theory, the truth lies not in any one poll but amid the preponderance of polls. Usually polls tend to bracket or straddle the results—some a bit high, some a bit low, with some right on the mark." A news organization that uses polls should report on all polls, not just its own, and should point out the variations in methods used by the different pollsters.

Unfortunately, journalists are often ignorant of the details of scientific polling. A recent study by political scientist Robert Y. Shapiro of

WRIGHT © *Palm Beach Post*. Distributed with permission by Tribune Media Services. All rights reserved.

Columbia University and University of Minnesota polling expert Lawrence R. Jacobs found that in the 296 newspaper, magazine, and TV reports they examined "about 80 percent of journalists' references to polls failed to offer the wording of questions, the responses to the alternatives presented in a question, and the error produced by sampling and other attributes of the survey." News organizations should seek out groups like the American Statistical Association, the American Association for Public Opinion Research, or the National Council on Public Polls to arrange cram courses for their reporters and editors.

In recent years there has been an explosion in scholarly explanations of the mysteries of polling. The information is shared within the academy and the profession. It is also imperative to let the public in on the secrets. An appropriate etiquette would be for news organizations to invent a regular poll-watch feature that would be as much a part of campaign reporting as the ad watch has become.

Polls
(for Politicians)

HOW DOES a president choose where to take his family on a summer vacation?

If the summer is 1995 and the president is Bill Clinton, the answer is that a pollster tells him where to go. At least this is the story that Dick Morris tells. "In a previous vacation, the president had gone to Martha's Vineyard, where photos of him on a yacht with Jacqueline Onassis did not help his populist image one bit," writes Morris. So next time the Clintons head for Wyoming and camping and hiking in the national parks. (Morris's subsequent opinion: "This advice was the ultimate in carrying polling to a mindless extreme.")

Presidents since Franklin Roosevelt have taken advice from pollsters. According to William Schneider, "Hadley Cantril showed President Roosevelt a poll [in 1935] revealing that if Louisiana Democratic Gov. Huey Long ran as a third-party candidate on a 'Share-the-Wealth' platform, he might take enough votes from the Democrats to deny the President reelection. When Roosevelt subsequently moved left, it was partly to co-opt the Long vote." And presidents since John Kennedy have had their own pollsters. But no president has made as much use of polling as Clinton.

The Little
Book of
Campaign
Etiquette

Robert Reich, Clinton's first secretary of labor, relates in a somewhat suspect memoir how the president uses polls to shape his agenda. Reich quotes the ubiquitous Morris as telling him to put his proposals in the administration's internal opinion polls: "Anything under forty percent doesn't work. Fifty percent is a possibility. Sixty or seventy, and the President may well use it." Clinton's staff counters that the president does not use polling to decide policies but as a tool for devising strategies that will get programs through Congress.

MACNELLY © *The Chicago Tribune.* Reprinted with permission of Jeff MacNelly. All rights reserved.

Polls, of course, can be a valuable means of taking the public's temperature. Our politicians are expected to factor our opinions into their decisions. But blind reliance on polls, *Wall Street Journal* columnist Albert R. Hunt reminds us, "would have rejected lend-lease and the draft prior to World War II, and the Marshall Plan after the war." As pollsters increasingly become part of politicians' inner circles, pollster David A. Paleologas warns that "leaders are more and more unwilling to take risks, unwilling to follow instincts, unwilling to be bold." Finger-to-the-wind decisionmaking is called pandering, not leadership. The etiquette of leadership should always ask (a) what is the right policy, (b) what is sound policy, (c) how can I convince my constituents of its rightness and soundness?

Predictions

A TV VIEWER ADVISORY: the political experts' predictions on *The McLaughlin Group* are wrong almost exactly as often as they are right. "The implication is clear," write the three scholars who did the tabulating. "Someone who tunes in *The McLaughlin Group* to get a better grip on the future would do just as well to flip a coin."

Weekends on television changed in 1981 when John McLaughlin, a former Jesuit priest and adviser to President Nixon, started a nationally syndicated talk show during which four Washington journalists, picked for their ideological fervor, begin each program by shouting at each other and end by making predictions.

The next year Cable News Network inaugurated the weekday *Crossfire* program, which further elevates the decibel level of what passes for conversation on TV. CNN added *Capital Gang* in 1988, CNBC initiated its version in 1989, and now Saturdays and Sundays on TV are a clutter of caustic Washington chatter. "One imagines the combatants being poked and provoked by their keepers before being unleashed," says Walter Goodman.

Although some of the participants are columnists (Bob Novak, Pat Buchanan, Michael Kinsley), a type of journalist employed specifically to announce his opinions, and some are professional politicians (John Sununu and Geraldine Ferraro), others are beat reporters, covering the White House or Congress or the courts, and thus expected by American journalism tradition to keep their opinions to themselves.

The long-standing Sunday fare—NBC's *Meet the Press,* CBS's *Face the Nation,* ABC's *This Week*—are programs in which reporters ask questions rather than answer them, but competition from the newcomers has forced them to add a concluding segment of opinionating journalists. The weekday morning network programs—*Today, Good Morning America*—have also added panels of Washington insiders (journalists and former politicians) to perform the same function.

Thus the fine distinction between opinion and "objective" journalism gets breached as journalists step across the line into what is essentially entertainment television. Journalists play at being celebrities, because, as Howard Kurtz notes, "To refuse to play the game is to risk appearing like a weenie."

The point is more than that these journalists' predictions are not very good. (There is empirical evidence that expert prediction in all fields is not very good.) The example of the TV journalist-entertainer is being felt throughout the news industry. Campaign reporting is now polluted by prediction. True, predictions are often put in the form of quotations from sources—politicians, scholars, pollsters—but they are there because reporters ask the questions and want the answers. According to an editor of the *American Journalism Review,* "No matter how political reporters try to hedge their predictions by tossing around phrases like 'if early indications are reliable,' and 'so far it seems,' and 'if polls are correct,' sooner or later their inability to predict human behavior becomes apparent."

"If you make predictions, you're going to make a fool of yourself," David Broder observes. "Generally, predictions aren't useful to readers or in the interest of good journalism." Journalists who worry about the state of their craft and their own reputations might recall this exchange between host Tim Russert and correspondent Lisa Myers on *Meet the Press* before the 1996 New Hampshire primary:

> *Russert: "What's your gut tell you?"*
> *Myers: "My gut tells me to keep my mouth shut."*

This is a response that deserves having a rule of etiquette named after it, the Myers Etiquette. When asked to predict, keep your mouth shut.

Push Polls

A PUSH POLL is a sleazy form of political campaigning in which a caller masquerades as a legitimate poll taker. It is not a poll at all but a form of telemarketing. This is how it works.

The accent is on volume and speed, make as many calls as possible and keep them short, typically thirty to sixty seconds. (Telephone industry competition has lowered unit cost so that this is now a moderately priced way to reach voters.) If the respondent favors your candidate, hang up quickly. If the respondent is for the other candidate or undecided, ask, "Would you vote for X if he had been convicted of drunk driving?" (Questions may rest on lies or may be out of context.) The objective is to push voters to vote against the caller's opponent. Calls are usually made forty-eight or seventy-two hours before election day so as to minimize opposition or media response. Callers either do not identify themselves or claim generic-sounding affiliations that are difficult to trace. One company employed by Bob Dole in 1996 used such names as National Market Share, National Research Center, and Campaign Telecommunications. In the words of a push poll advocate, "Negative phoning leaves few footprints."

Push polls (more formally known as "negative persuasion" or "advocacy phoning") are used by candidates from both parties, generally in tight races for the U.S. House of Representatives where the constituency is small and defined and the urgency for taking votes away from an opponent is great. But by 1994 push polls were also being employed in statewide gubernatorial and Senate races, notably against Oliver North in Virginia and Jeb Bush in Florida.

During 1996 negative persuasion polls were alleged to have been sighted in the Iowa caucuses and the New Hampshire primary. Steve Forbes in Iowa accused the Dole campaign of hiring a Utah telemarketing firm to do push polling on his abortion and gay rights positions. In New Hampshire Dole callers asked if voters would be more or less inclined to vote for Pat Buchanan if they knew he once said that women lacked "ambition and the will to succeed." Dole's people insist that these calls were performing legitimate campaign research.

The National Council on Public Polls, an association of major polling firms, and the American Association for Public Opinion Research, the leading association of scholars in the field, worries that these efforts to disguise negative campaign tactics as survey research damage the reputation of legitimate polling and discourage people from participating in their surveys. The American Association of Political Consultants declares push polls in violation of its stricture against "any activity which would corrupt or degrade the practice of political campaigning."

Obviously negative campaigning did not start with push polls. As Adam Clymer writes, "In the 1940s, 'midnight fliers' would appear on doorsteps on Election Eve, anonymously accusing candidates of such sins as having Communist friends, dating Negroes, or conspiring with the Pope." But a telephone call is a most personal communication—one voice connecting with another—and thus a more effective means of campaigning than strewing doorsteps with fliers. And because office seekers employ whatever techniques have been successful in the past, negative persuasion polls will grow in popularity among the political class.

Congressman Thomas Petri (R-Wis.) has proposed requiring disclosure when push polls are used. At the end of the interview the caller must identity the person paying for the poll. The person who conducts the poll must report its cost and the source of the funds to the Federal Election Commission. The person who conducts the poll must also report the number of households contacted if more than 400 and must file a copy of the poll questions. The law presently mandates that print and electronic publications and advertisements reveal their sponsorship, and Petri's proposals for telephone bank operators is not dissimilar.

Larry Sabato and Glenn Simpson in *Dirty Little Secrets: The Persistence of Corruption in American Politics* note the difficulty of stamping out the growing push poll phenomenon for First Amendment reasons and because of the problem of distinguishing sleaze from legitimate research polls. They too opt for disclosure and stiff penalties to "punish the guilty." Ultimately, however, this form of telemarketing will stop only when purveyors see that it no longer works. And this can best happen when enough people notify local TV stations and newspapers, as well as the headquarters of slandered candidates, to register disgust with a telephone call that bears the hallmarks of a negative persuasion poll.

Revolving Door

WHAT DO George Stephanopoulos and Susan Molinari have in common? *They were both government officials who are now journalists.* What do Sidney Blumenthal and Strobe Talbott have in common? *They were both journalists who are now government officials.* What do David Gergen and Pat Buchanan have in common? *They were both government officials who became journalists who became government officials who are now journalists.*

You get the idea. It's called the revolving door. Players are called revolvers.

Some think it's terrible. Max Frankel sees "the progressive collapse of the walls that traditionally separated news from propaganda." Alicia C. Shepard writes that "jumping back and forth hurts journalism's credibility, a commodity already in tatters." Once the press "loses its distinctive identity," David Broder, the most outspoken critic of revolvers, has said "it will not be long before we lose our freedom." (Buchanan calls Broder a "sermonizing, sanctimonious prig.")

Others are enthusiastic. Carl T. Rowan: "This country would be a helluva lot better off if every newspaper and magazine editor, every television news director or station manager, spent a few years inside government." William Safire, former speechwriter for Richard Nixon and now a Pulitzer Prize–winning columnist for the *New York Times,* concludes that those who switch roles "gain stereoscopic perspective from looking through one political and one journalistic eye. The ironic nuance is hard to explain to one who has never been on the other side of the barricades."

Whether good or bad, or a little of both, there is more revolving now

WASSERMAN © *The Boston Globe*. Distributed by the Los Angeles Times Syndicate.

than in the past and there will be still more in the future. Partly this is because news organizations have changed their rules and are willing to take back or hire journalists after they work in government and political campaigns. But mainly it is because TV wants celebrities to fill the ranks of its news shows and doesn't care where name recognition comes from.

Part of the problem is definitional. *Reporter* and *correspondent* are titles that imply fact diggers, objective unbiased members of the press; *columnist* and *commentator* are titles that come with a license to express opinions, even prejudices. Yet all are called *journalists.* Pat Buchanan says, "I'm a journalist by profession, whose hobby is running for office." If Buchanan instead declared, "I'm a newspaper columnist and TV commentator, whose hobby . . . ," much of the sting could be taken out of the controversy, which basically confuses opinion givers with fact diggers. "Hell, everybody knows the Buchanan agenda, whether he is in the White House or writing a column," opines fellow columnist Carl Rowan. "Nobody is deceived."

What is needed is an etiquette:

—Nonjournalists hired by news organizations should be given commentator or columnist positions. Part of the upset in the journalism world comes when CBS makes Congresswoman Molinari an anchor, an assignment usually associated with fact diggers, or when ABC hires presidential assistant Stephanopoulos as a correspondent. Objective journalism is not like medicine or law for which you need a license, and occasionally a former politician has done brilliantly, as has Tim Russert, who came to NBC from being an aide to New York Governor Mario Cuomo, but this should be judged exceptional.

—Politicians who are hired as commentators and columnists should be labeled and identified by their previous jobs, parties, or ideology at least until they are better known as journalists than as former government officials. A statute of limitations decrees that there comes a time when it is unnecessary to say that Bill Moyers was Lyndon Johnson's press secretary.

—Journalists returning to journalism after government or political service (a) should not be immediately assigned to cover those who have been their colleagues and (b) should know that they are being carefully scrutinized by their superiors. This is as much for their professional protection as for their organizations'.

Sex Scandals

ADULTERY HAS become part of the regular menu of topics subject to presidential campaign reporting.

The 1988 election campaign. U.S. Senator Gary Hart, candidate for the Democratic nomination, has a reputation as a womanizer. It is in this context that he tells E. J. Dionne Jr., "Follow me around. I don't care. I'm serious. If somebody wants to put a tail on me, go ahead. They'd be very bored." Dionne's article appears in the *New York Times Magazine* on May 3, 1987. On the same day, based on accounts by reporters who have been tailing Hart, the *Miami Herald* reports he is spending a weekend alone in his Washington townhouse with a Miami model named Donna Rice. The candidate's wife stands by him. "In all honesty," says Lee Hart, "if it doesn't bother me, I don't think it ought to bother anyone else. But the *Washington Post* editorializes, "Mr. Hart has been open, explicit and audacious in his denial of rumors of playing around. He is running for president. He has made his veracity on this question a kind of test of his general truthfulness." A photograph soon surfaces showing Hart and Rice boarding a boat called "Monkey Business." With one question— "Have you ever committed adultery?" asked by reporter Paul Taylor at Hart's press conference on May 6, 1987—a new era begins in U.S. press behavior and politics. The *Post* informs Hart it has information of other liaisons and he drops out of the race, charging the press with making a mockery of the election process.

The 1992 election campaign. Shortly before the New Hampshire primary, Gennifer Flowers of Little Rock tells the *Star,* a supermarket tabloid, that she has had a twelve-year affair with Arkansas Governor Bill Clinton. She is pronounced damaged goods by some journalists because she sold her story to the paper (reputedly for $50,000). But it comes with tapes of incriminating telephone conversations. Clinton and wife Hillary make their case in a *60 Minutes* interview. The candidate acknowledges "causing pain in my marriage." He doesn't provide details, but notes, "Anybody who's listening gets the drift of it." His wife adds, "If that's not enough for people, then heck, don't vote for him." Reporters' responses are generally sympathetic, partly perhaps in reaction to the gumshoe treatment they gave Hart.

Later in 1992 the front page of the *New York Post* headlines "THE BUSH AFFAIR." A writer claims a U.S. ambassador once said he arranged for Vice President George Bush to share a private cottage with a female aide during a 1984 visit to Geneva. Now president and running for reelection, Bush denies the accusation. He does not have a womanizer reputation. The ambassador is dead. It is not a difficult decision for responsible news organizations to decline to publish this unproven story.

The 1996 election campaign. Ten days before the election a supermarket tabloid, the *National Enquirer,* reveals that a suburban Washington woman admits having had an affair with Bob Dole four years before he divorced his first wife in 1972. As with the tale of Bush's alleged adultery, the mainstream press rejects the story. Yet there is a difference: Bush's liaison is unsubstantiated rumor; Dole's is documented in preelection investigations by *Time* and the *Washington Post.*

Why do the news media turn their collective backs on the story of a candidate's proven extramarital affair? The answer stems more from

the situation than from a moral reawakening. Editors kill this story
for some or all of five reasons: (1) a statute of limitations (the affair
ended twenty-eight years before); (2) a tacit salute to Dole, who has
not made an issue of his opponent's private behavior; (3) respect for
the woman in question, who refuses money for her story and only
wants to be left alone; (4) a judgment that the revelation comes too

WASSERMAN © *The Boston Globe.* Distributed by the Los Angeles Times Syndicate.

close to election day; and (5) an assessment that Dole is going to lose the election anyway.

Max Frankel, former executive editor of the *New York Times,* suggests that the cold war once gave American journalists an excuse to pry into the lives of politicians who were "potential targets for blackmail by the Soviet secret police." Yet the end of the cold war obviously doesn't ensure that the next election's sex scandal will be unreported in the mainstream media. Competition and technology continue to blur the lines between trash and traditional journalism. Once stories turn up in the tabloids or on talk radio or in cyberspace, the only fire walls that can keep them out of daily newspapers or off network television are journalists' ethical judgments.

The Paula Jones and Monica Lewinsky controversies have whetted the media's appetite for political titillation and underlined the danger, in the words of columnist Gerald F. Seib, that the press will "plunge into the 2000 presidential race without having put in place any guardrails [and thus] open the way for all manner of journalistic excesses."

One of the basic principles of a code of ethics approved by the Society of Professional Journalists in 1996 is to "minimize harm." When, then, are reporters justified in reporting a politician's sex life? Based on the sensible thoughts of the *Wall Street Journal's* Albert R. Hunt, here is an etiquette defining a set of conditions that make private information pertinent in campaign coverage:

—if the candidate lies,

—if the relationship is of recent vintage or is still continuing,

—if the relationship directly affects the politician's public life or governing decisions,

—if there's "blatant hypocrisy" such as the candidate's running on a platform of restoring morality in America.

Sound Bites

PRESIDENTIAL CANDIDATES' sound bites appearing on the network evening news programs have shrunk from 43.1 seconds in 1968 to 25.2 seconds in 1972 to 18.2 seconds in 1976 to 9.8 seconds in 1988 to 7.2 seconds by early 1996. What's going on?

As presidential campaign stories become shorter, the percentage of the stories in which the journalists are speaking (rather than the candidates) becomes bigger and the percentage of journalists expressing opinions (rather than giving information) also increases.

Let's compare two representative network TV stories from the 1968 and 1988 presidential campaigns. The first report was seen on the *CBS Evening News* with Walter Cronkite, October 8, 1968:

Cronkite: Hubert Humphrey said today that the nuclear age calls for new forms of diplomacy, and he suggested regular summit meetings with the Soviet Union. He made his proposal to a meeting of the nation's newspaper editors and publishers in Washington.

Humphrey speaks for 1 minute 26 seconds.

Cronkite: Humphrey was asked about the battered state of the Democratic party.

Humphrey speaks for 49 seconds.

Twenty years later, September 28, 1988, another presidential campaign story, this time from ABC and Peter Jennings:

Jennings: Well, it was a shirt-sleeved George Bush who added a bit of country flavor to his campaign today. ABC's Brit Hume was with him.

Hume: The Bush campaign rolled up the spine of Illinois today in a bus caravan intended to portray the vice president as a man in tune with rural America. Indeed, the tunes were supplied by country music stars Loretta Lynn, Crystal Gayle, and Peggy Sue.

They sing "Stand by George Bush" to the tune of "Stand by Your Man" for 9 seconds.

Hume: Bush's bus, by the way, had a microwave oven, a fancy restroom, and, best of all, no reporters. They now travel with Bush, but not near him. At a series of small town rallies, a shirt-sleeved Bush was introduced by Loretta Lynn. He told folks he was with them, unlike the other guy who wants to tighten tax collection to cut the deficit $35 billion, something Bush said would require doubling the Internal Revenue force.

Bush speaks for 19 seconds.

Hume: Earlier, Bush also worked the IRS into an attack on Dukakis's college loan plan, which would be financed by continuing payments much like social security.

Bush speaks for 7 seconds.

Hume: Polls show Bush behind in Illinois and he apparently thought getting out among the people would be just the thing. Did that also mean he would answer reporters' questions? Not today.

After all, you can carry this accessibility stuff too far. Brit Hume, ABC News, Ottawa, Illinois.

Two observations. TV news stories now are faster paced and more entertaining. News stories then were more substantive. Brevity, of course, can be a virtue. The Ten Commandments contain fewer than a

'...Political campaigns have become so simplistic and superficial... In the 20 seconds we have left, could you explain why?..

hundred words. As a journalism professor has noted, "Politicians can produce four sentences of empty rhetoric as easily as one." However, when the Center for Media and Public Affairs examined candidates' pronouncements and network news during the 1996 New Hampshire primary, it found that the candidates were three times as substantive as media coverage.

The trade-off—substance for style—relates to technological and economic changes in the television business. Replacing film with tape in news reporting creates the opportunity for instant editing. (Putting together all of the pieces that made up Brit Hume's 1988 package would not have been possible for a comparable story in 1968.) Moreover, in the cable TV era, with the average viewer being offered forty-seven choices, the networks believe they need a faster-paced news product to meet the competition. This product features enhanced roles for star anchors and correspondents and the shorter sound bites.

By 1996 there may have been some public reaction. A Kaiser Family Foundation survey found that 77 percent of respondents say they would rather hear positions on issues from the candidates themselves. Only 16 percent say they prefer reporters to explain those positions. (But Richard Wald, senior vice president of ABC News, says, "If you believe surveys that ask people what they watch on TV, PBS is the highest-rated network in the world and ballet is huge.")

Whether candidates invented snappy sound bites first—to force TV to take their messages in a form that their consultants believe showed them to most advantage—or whether the candidates are merely responding to TV's demand for shorter sound bites if they wish to be seen, is something of a chicken-or-egg proposition. In either case the result is that voters see less of their presidential candidates talking about serious issues on TV news.

The pendulum has swung too far. News programs are supposed to be about newsmakers, not news reporters. It's the politician who runs for president. Voters need know a great deal more about what the candidate stands for than about what the journalist thinks. The TV journalist's etiquette? Ask not what this story can do for your career, ask rather is this the most help I can give viewers when they enter the voting booth.

Straw Polls

LONG BEFORE the Iowa caucuses and the New Hampshire primary—the formal start of the presidential campaign—there is the "invisible primary" as potential aspirants to the White House maneuver for position. One element of the ritual is participation in straw polls, so-called, apparently, from "throwing straws into the wind" to see which way it is blowing.

The best known of these are sponsored by state party committees and are designed as fund-raisers. Buy a ticket, get a vote. The price may be $25 or $50. Some voters are from out of state. Some candidates pay for the tickets. One campaign operative complains that her party has "reinvented the poll tax." Nothing scientific about these polls.

Nor is there anything predictive. Political scientist Emmett Buell has added up the results of eighteen state straw polls between 1975 and 1991 and concludes that the eventual nominees won only nine times. Victory in a state's straw poll does not even ensure victory in that state's primary or caucus. Ask Phil Gramm. He invested heavily in the 1995 Louisiana straw poll, won, then lost the state's primary the next year, effectively ending his race for the Republican nomination.

Most national party leaders agree with Charles Manatt, who when chairman of the Democratic National Committee denounced straw polls as "divisive, nonuseful, expensive, and extraordinarily irritating." His party banned them in the run-up to the 1988 nomination, but they were back by the next election cycle.

These pseudoevents are eagerly awaited by political reporters, particularly in off-off years, such as 1983 or 1995, when there are few elections to engage them. One 1983 straw poll of 124 Alabama Young Democrats, won by Alan Cranston (65 votes), was reported on all three TV networks. According to ABC, the outcome gave "an added touch of credibility" to Cranston's candidacy. The *Washington Post* devoted 7,117 words to pre-1996 straw poll stories. On June 26, 1994, it reported, "It's official. The Republicans have a front-runner, sort of"—based on 1,349 votes in an Iowa straw poll. In the next year's Iowa straw poll Dole and Gramm each get 2,582 votes—at $25 a vote—and the *Post* concluded that this "provided the first small chink in the veil of invincibility that Dole has sought to drape around his candidacy."

Local politicians are not going to abandon the straw poll. Why should they? They are seen on television and quoted in the press. But is this a good enough reason to continue an inane practice? Etiquette here should be that any event staged exclusively for the media is not worth serious attention from the media.

Talk Radio

TALK RADIO has come of age. The number of stations in the United States using a news/talk format is well over a thousand, up from 360 in 1990. Twenty-three percent of Americans say they listened to talk radio either yesterday or today. "Talk Radio has become a staple in the diet of about one in six Americans," a 1993 survey concludes.

Listeners look very much like the nation as a whole except they are twice as likely to be conservatives as liberals. "The dominant theme" of talk radio, writes Katharine Q. Seelye, "is that government is too big and too intrusive and does unbelievably dumb things." The leitmotifs are complaints about the "liberal news media" and a visceral contempt for the Clintons. "It's as obvious as the nose on your face," Gordon Liddy tells his listeners. "The guy could shoot Hillary at high noon out on Pennsylvania Avenue and [the press]would say she got mugged. [They] cover up for him. Why? Because he is a leftist." According to Michael Harrison, editor of *Talkers* magazine, "Bill Clinton is the most criticized individual in the history of the medium." Hillary Clinton is second; Saddam Hussein, third.

Claims for talk radio's political impact rise and fall with the success of conservatives on Election Day. After the Republicans captured the U.S.

House of Representatives in 1994, the party's freshmen legislators made Rush Limbaugh an honorary member of their class. "I would not be here except for talk radio," claimed Senator James F. Inhofe (R-Okla.). Less was heard of talk radio's clout when Clinton won reelection two years later. "I think people have wildly exaggerated talk radio's impact on the '94 campaign, and those who say it had no effect whatever in this [1996] campaign are also probably wrong," says William Adams, publisher of *Talk Daily*. "It's a small but significant part of the media equation." Adams believes talk radio is likely to have greatest impact in Republican primaries during presidential campaigns and during off-year elections when turnout is lower.

Issues with a strong populist tilt also show talk radio's effectiveness, as when Congress proposed giving itself a 50 percent pay raise, the House Bank scandal broke, term limits were debated, and in 1993 when attorney general–designate Zoe Baird admitted hiring illegal aliens to care for her children and failing to pay the required social security taxes. A headline in the *Washington Post* concluded "BAIRD'S HIRING DISCLOSURE NOT SEEN AS MAJOR BLOCK"; radio talkers correctly thought otherwise.

Talk shows are no place for namby-pambies. "It's certainty of opinion that dictates the selection of on-air personalities," says talk show host Brian Lehrer. And hosts' ratings reflect the edge to their opinions. Some go over the edge. Mike Siegel of Seattle's KVI repeats an allegation that Mayor Norm Rice has been shot by his wife while engaging in a homosexual act. Richard Clear of KGA, Spokane, questions whether Congressman Thomas Foley is a homosexual.

Talk radio has acquired many of the trappings of a profession: its own association awards, an industry magazine, a newsletter on program content. Programs are now taken very seriously by communications scholars. Susan Herbst of Northwestern University comments, "It would be naive to think that they will bring us true participatory democracy. But the potential for unstructured expression is far greater here than with conventional media."

While this is entertainment, not journalism, it's entertainment that has public policy consequences. As such, rather than peer review—something like a news council sitting in judgment—talk radio's etiquette is most appropriately equal time, giving those who have been attacked the last word.

The Little Book of Campaign Etiquette

Vocabulary

FRANK LUNTZ, who advises Republican politicians on the words they should use, says, "Words are everything. They can declare war or define a peace. They can soothe or inflame. . . . We have found the words and phrases that will move the American people." If his clients want to eliminate the estate tax, he recommends they substitute the phrase "death tax." Everyone dies, but only the rich have estates.

Even though politicians' vocabulary changes over time, populist words always trump elitist words in a democracy. We require journalists as our guides. Keep us informed: *compromise* is bad, *negotiate* is good; *rhetoric* is bad, *dialogue* is good; *promises* are bad, *principles* are good; *partisan* bad, *independent* good. Our side has *freedom fighters;* their side has *terrorists.*

Special is usually an elevating word: special friends are the most valued, special deliveries come the fastest, special forces are the bravest. Yet *special* is bad in the political vocabulary when it comes before *interests.* "Call Congressman [name]. Tell him to protect our kids, not special interests," says the sound track on a generic AFL-CIO commercial. The congressman replies by attacking the AFL-CIO as a special interest.

Reform is the slipperiest word in the politician's lexicon. Geneva

Overholser, the *Washington Post*'s ombudsman, worries about its usage: "health care reform, welfare reform, immigration reform. Would all agree that whatever is offered under these labels is an improvement? Reform is no valueless word, not just change, but change for the better."

Meg Greenfield, a journalist who has spent many years watching politicians pin labels on donkeys and elephants, also reminds us that all reforms have time limits on them, that is, "the number of years it will take for motivated people to learn how to manipulate the reform to their

advantage," and all reforms are "in some way flawed" (which does not mean that no improvements can be made).

When on June 16, 1972, operatives of Richard Nixon's Committee to Reelect the President (known as CREEP) broke into the offices of the Democratic National Committee, located in a downtown Washington building complex (known as Watergate), they not only inaugurated the most serious political scandal in American history, they also created a cliche that has polluted politics for a quarter-century.

The *American Journalism Review* in 1997 listed fifteen "scandals, semi-scandals and pseudoscandals" to which *gate* is affixed: Billygate, Debategate, Filegate, Gurugate, Hillarygate, Indogate (also known as Lippogate, Huanggate, and Donorgate), Irangate (also known as Olliegate and Contragate), Iraqgate, Nannygate, Newtgate, Passportgate, Rubbergate, Travelgate (followed by FBIgate), Troopergate (also known as Paulagate and Pantsgate), and Whitewatergate. Another year, 1998, another set of gates. *New York Times* columnist and lexicographer William Safire, who does a lot of gating, says, "If I ever get to heaven, watch for Pearlygate." By adding *gate* to a malfeasance of any size or shape, all scandals have been cheapened.

Politicians can claim reforms to their hearts' content. Who's against reform? They can be against special interests and for dialogue. The journalists' etiquette is to warn about the political word traps that have been set for us.

Voters

LESS THAN HALF of Americans eligible to cast a ballot for president did so in 1996, the lowest turnout since Calvin Coolidge was elected. But in 1924 women had just been enfranchised and were not yet voting at the same rate as men. Otherwise, we have to go back to 1824 (Adams-Jackson-Crawford-Clay) to find a presidential contest in which there was so little voter interest.

The 1996 results were particularly disappointing because there were good reasons to expect the vote percentage to increase. The so-called motor-voter law added millions of potential new voters. States such as Oregon and Washington were making it easier to vote by mail. And more Americans—the baby boomers—were now in the midlife age group most likely to vote.

The results are even more discouraging in off-year or midterm elections. In one of these years only a third of the eligible voters will make it to the polls.

Will there come an election when nobody shows up? This question troubled President Kennedy, who appointed a commission in 1963 to find answers. The experts concluded that too many Americans are not voting because our system makes it too difficult. So they proposed ending literacy tests as a requisite for voting, outlawing the poll tax, lowering the voting age to 18, and making it easier for citizens to register to vote. Every recommendation has now been adopted. The result? A steady decrease in voting percentage (with one upward blip in 1992).

Experts no longer believe legal barriers cause the United States to have the lowest turnout of any nation for which there are reliable numbers. While there are still ways to make voting easier—hold elections on Sundays or make Election Day a holiday, eliminate all voter registration—changes in process will not suddenly turn us into a nation of voters.

What are other reasons given for our condition of nonvoting?

—*The Twenty-Sixth Amendment.* By adding 18-, 19-, and 20-year-old voters by constitutional amendment in 1970 we automatically lowered the national participation rate since the young are least apt to go to the polls. "This does not suggest that the newly enfranchised voters account for all of the decline," according to researchers at the University of Illinois, "but they quite clearly account for a considerable portion of the post-1968 deterioration."

—*Weakened parties.* Political organizations used to be responsible for getting voters to the polls on Election Day.

—*Uninspiring candidates.* The heavier turnout in 1992 is partly attributed to excitement generated by Ross Perot.

—*Negative advertising.* In one experimental model, scholars found that negative advertising decreases by 5 percent the share of those intending to vote, but this is questioned by other scholars. In short, experts disagree on why Americans don't vote.

What is wrong with not voting anyway? John Adams wrote his wife Abigail, "I must study politics and war that my sons may have liberty to study mathematics and philosophy. My sons ought to study mathematics and philosophy . . . in order to give their children a right to study painting, poetry, music, architecture." Our second president had his priorities right. Politics is a necessary but not exalted calling. Still, the act of voting is the most modest act of uncoerced citizenship in a democracy. Curtis Gans points out, "People who don't vote tend not to participate in any other aspect of civic life, which means that as voting rates decline, the reservoir of volunteers for socially useful tasks also declines."

This little book often finds fault with politicians and journalists. I also fault the systems through which we elect presidents. But the systems are open to those who have the will and the energy and the intelligence to

The Little Book of Campaign Etiquette

change them. And, unlike the nonvoters, the vast majority of politicians and journalists still care about the public life of the United States.

What of the nonvoters? Once they were the least educated. Now there is little difference demographically between those who vote and those who do not. Indeed, the largest absolute drop in voting is in the nation's wealthier suburbs, home to the well educated. We cannot blame our teachers for the half of us who have lost the sense of civic engagement.

It is time to look in the mirror.

Winning and Losing

WE CAST OUR BALLOTS. The votes are counted. The lights go out at the polling places. Yet there is still one last ritual to perform before the campaign is over. The loser gives a concession speech and the winner a victory speech (in that order).

For the winner, the question is how to frame euphoria. For the loser, "the rhetorical challenge is to portray one's own defeat as a chapter of honor in the nation's history, to put a brave face on failure, transforming defeat into a semblance of victory." It is no mean feat to do this so soon after an event of public rejection.

Aficionados of the genre always give highest honors to Governor Adlai Stevenson of Illinois in 1952:

> *The people have rendered their verdict and I gladly accept it. General Eisenhower has been a great leader in war. He has been a vigorous and valiant opponent in this campaign. . . . It is traditionally American to fight hard before an election. It is equally traditional to close ranks as soon as the people have spoken.*
>
> *From the depths of my heart I thank all of my party and all of those independents and Republicans who supported Senator Sparkman and me.*

That which unites us as American citizens is far greater than that which divides us as political parties. I urge you all to give General Eisenhower the support he will need to carry out the great tasks that lie before him. I pledge him mine.

We vote as many, but we pray as one. With a united people, with faith in democracy, with common concern for others less fortunate around the globe, we shall move forward with God's guidance toward the time when His children shall grow in freedom and dignity in a world at peace.

Someone asked me, as I came in, down on the street, how I felt, and I was reminded of a story that a fellow townsman of ours used to tell— Abraham Lincoln. They asked him how he felt once after an unsuccessful election. He said he felt like a little boy who had stubbed his toe in the dark. He said that he was too old to cry but it hurt too much to laugh.

Not every election night loser or winner will be able to be as eloquent as Stevenson. But all candidates should be able to follow this etiquette:

—*Give thanks.* The list can be short or long. It is optional to thank spouse and children, campaign staff, contributors, volunteers. But it is mandatory to thank the voters. To do otherwise is poor form. The morning after Herbert Hoover lost in 1932 he held a press conference:

Q. "Mr. President, is there anything you want to say to the people who supported you? I noticed you didn't say anything last night."

A. "I haven't had time. I just got up. I probably will say something."

—*Be gracious.* Nobody loves a braggart or a whiner. Particularly in defeat. The morning after losing the race for governor of California in 1962, Richard Nixon strode into a press conference called by an aide to concede his defeat:

*Good morning, gentlemen. Now that all the members of the press are so
delighted that I have lost, I'd like to make a statement of my own. . . .*

*I congratulate Governor Brown. . . . I believe Governor Brown has
a heart, even though he believes I do not. I believe he is a good
American, even though he feels I am not. . . .*

*The press [should] first recognize the great responsibility they have
to report all the news and, second, recognize that they have a right and
a responsibility, if they're against a candidate, to give him the shaft,
but also recognize if they give him the shaft, put one lonely reporter on
the campaign who will report what the candidate says now and then.*

—*Think strategic.* Words in victory or defeat have consequences. In
1980 President Carter gave his concession speech at 9:54 p.m. He was
disappointed, of course, and must have wanted to get away from the
Sheraton Washington Hotel as quickly as possible. But it was not even
7:00 p.m. on the West Coast; the polls were still open. According to
observers, some potential voters decided to stay at home, causing several
Democratic congressmen to claim Carter's hasty words caused their
defeat. Stevenson's graceful exit in 1952, on the other hand, helped to
keep the door open to renomination four years later.

—*Be brief* (unlike Ross Perot, who turned his 1992 concession speech
into a singing and dancing jamboree). It's been a long day. A lot of people are staying up to hear these final words. As citizens, we have earned
the right to be tired. America's long election cycle once again comes full
circle.

It is time to say good night.

I TOLD YOU SO! Reprinted with permission of Charles Bissell. All rights reserved.

For Additional Information

Advertising (for Consumers)
Annenberg School of Communication, University of Pennsylvania, *Tracking the Quality of 1996 Campaign Discourse,* especially nos. 1, 2, 8, 17 (September 9–November 4, 1996).
Department of Communication, University of Oklahoma, "Special 1996 Election Issue," *Political Advertising Research Reports,* vol. 3 (Summer 1997).
L. Patrick Devlin, "Contrasts in Presidential Campaign Commercials of 1996," *American Behavioral Scientist,* vol. 40 (August 1997).
Kathleen Hall Jamieson, *Dirty Politics: Deception, Distraction, and Democracy* (Oxford University Press, 1992).
William G. Mayer, "In Defense of Negative Campaigning," *Political Science Quarterly,* vol. 111 (Fall 1996).

Advertising (for Journalists)
Stephen Ansolabehere and Shanto Iyengar, "Can the Press Monitor Campaign Advertising?" *Harvard International Journal of Press/ Politics,* vol. 1 (Winter 1996).

Courtney Bennet, "Assessing the Impact of Ad Watches on the Strategic Decision-Making Process," *American Behavioral Scientist,* vol. 40 (August 1997).

Edwin Diamond, Maja Holkebore, and Lisa Sandberg, "Press Monitoring of Campaign Ads Probably Didn't Make a Difference," *National Journal,* November 11, 1996.

Kathleen Hall Jamieson and Joseph N. Cappella, "Setting the Record Straight: Do Ad Watches Help or Hurt?" *Harvard International Journal of Press/Politics,* vol. 2 (Winter 1997).

Michael A. Milburn and Justin Brown, "Busted by the Ad Police: Journalists' Coverage of Political Campaign Ads in the 1992 Presidential Campaign," research paper R-15, Shorenstein Center, Harvard University, July 1995.

Martha T. Moore, "Political Ads: The Camera Can Tell Lies," *USA Today,* May 23, 1996.

Martin Schram, "How the Media Can Negate the Negative TV Ads," *The Hill,* February 21, 1996.

John C. Tedesco, Lori Melton McKinnon, and Lynda Lee Kaid, "Advertising Watchdogs: A Content Analysis of Print and Broadcast Ad Watches," *Harvard International Journal of Press/Politics,* vol. 1 (Fall 1996).

Advertising (for Politicians)

Curtis Gans, "Stop the Madness!" *Washington Monthly,* May 1997.

Karen S. Johnson-Cartee and Gary A. Copeland, *Negative Political Advertising: Coming of Age* (Hillsdale, N.J.: Lawrence Erlbaum Associates, 1991).

Rushworth M. Kidder, "In Maine, a 'Code of Election Ethics' Curbs Negative Campaigning," *Boston Sunday Globe,* October 20, 1996.

Robert Spero, *The Duping of the American Voter* (Lippincott & Crowell, 1980).

Darrell M. West, *Air Wars*, 2d ed. (Washington: Congressional Quarterly Press, 1997).

Anonymous Sources

Robert G. Kaiser, "When Unnamed Sources Are Necessary," *Washington Post*, March 14, 1997.

Geneva Overholser, "Who Said That?" *Washington Post*, February 18, 1996; "Rejecting Anonymity," *Washington Post*, March 10, 1996; "Naming Sources," *Washington Post*, March 9, 1997.

A. H. Raskin, "Who Said That? A Report to the National News Council on the Use of Unidentified Sources," 1983.

Lori Robertson, "A Public Debate over Unnamed Sources," *American Journalism Review* (May 1997).

Bias

David Broder, "Interview," *Miller Center Journal*, vol. 4 (Spring 1997).

Everett E. Dennis, "The Myth of the Liberal Slant," *American Editor* (January–February 1997).

S. Robert Lichter, "Consistently Liberal: But Does It Matter?" *Forbes MediaCritic*, vol. 4 (Fall 1996).

Geneva Overholser, "The Battle against Bias," *Washington Post*, May 10, 1998.

William Powers, "Scandal-Shy," *New Republic*, December 16, 1996.

Paul Starobin, "Heeding the Call," *National Journal*, November 30, 1996.

Robert P. Vallone, Lee Ross, and Mark R. Lepper, "The Hostile Media Phenomena: Biased Perception and Perception of Media Bias in Coverage of the Beirut Massacre," *Journal of Personality and Social Psychology*, vol. 49, no. 3 (1985).

David H. Weaver and G. Cleveland Wilhoit, *The American Journalists in the 1990s* (Mahwah, N.J.: Lawrence Erlbaum Associates, 1996).

Conflict of Interest
Michael Kinsley, "The Conflict-of-Interest Craze," *Washington Monthly,* November 1978.
Eric Mink, "Bar Chuck from All Political Stories!" *New York Daily News,* February 27, 1996.
"The Political Spouse Issue," *Editor & Publisher,* March 30, 1996.
George F. Will, "A Story of Ethics and Family Values," *Washington Post,* March 17, 1996.

Consultants (for Candidates)
James Bennet, "The New Campaign Story: Consultants Steal Spotlight," *New York Times,* September 9, 1996.
Frank I. Luntz, *Candidates, Consultants, and Campaigns* (Basil Blackwell, 1988).
Dick Morris, *Behind the Oval Office* (Random House, 1997).
Ed Rollins, *Bare Knuckles and Back Rooms* (Broadway Books, 1966).
Larry J. Sabato, *The Rise of Political Consultants* (Basic Books, 1981).

Consultants (for Journalists)
Tucker Carlson, "The Consultant Culture," *Weekly Standard,* November 4, 1996.
Jerry Hagstrom, "The Consulting Shuffle," *National Journal,* November 1, 1996.
Howard Kurtz, "GOP Consultant's Strategy: Label Opponents Liberally," *Washington Post,* October 22, 1996.

Peter Levine, "Do Political Consultants Harm the Electoral Process?" *CQ Researcher,* vol. 6 (October 4, 1996).

Patrick Novotny and Richard H. Jacobs, "Geographical Information Systems and the New Landscape of Political Technologies," *Social Science Computer Review,* vol. 15 (Fall 1997).

Michael Rust, "Manipulating the Candidate," *Insight,* March 10, 1997.

Peter H. Stone, "Man with a Message [Frank Luntz]," *Nationnal Journal,* April 19, 1997.

Conventions

Edwin Diamond, Gregg Geller, and Chris Whitley, "Air Wars: Conventions Go Cable," *National Journal Convention Special,* August 31, 1996.

Jonathan Karl, "Covering the Conventions Inside and Out," *Media Studies Journal,* vol. 11 (Winter 1997).

Gerald C. Lubenow, "IGS Observer," *Public Affairs Report,* Institute of Governmental Studies, University of California–Berkeley (September 1996).

Jim Naureckas, "Koppel Copped Out at Convention," *Extra! Update* (October 1996).

Nelson W. Polsby and Aaron Wildavsky, *Presidential Elections: Strategies and Structures of American Politics,* 9th ed. (Chatham House, 1996).

Corrections

Bill Monroe, "Grave Mistakes" (letter to the editor), *Columbia Journalism Review* (May–June 1997).

Geneva Overholser, "The Ways of Our Errors," *Washington Post,* November 26, 1995.

Emerson Stone, "On-Air Corrections," *Communicator,* vol. 9 (March 1995).

D. Charles Whitney, "Begging Your Pardon: Corrections and Corrections Policies at Twelve U.S. Newspapers," New York: Gannett Center for Media Studies, 1986.

Cyberpolitics

Anthony Corrado and Charles M. Firestone, eds., *Elections in Cyberspace: Toward a New Era in American Politics* (Washington: Aspen Institute, 1996).

Freedom Forum Media Studies Center, "Cybercampaigns Preach to the Choir," The Media & Campaign '96 Briefing (April 1996).

Andrew J. Glass, "On-line Elections: The Internet's Impact on the Political Process," *Harvard International Journal of Press/Politics,* vol. 1 (Fall 1996).

Doris A. Graber, "The 'New' Media and Politics: What Does the Future Hold?" *PS,* vol. 29 (March 1996).

J. D. Lasica, "Net Gain," *American Journalism Review* (November 1996).

Douglas Muzio and David Birdsell, "The 1996 'Net Voter," *Public Perspective* (December-January 1997).

Pew Research Center for The People & The Press, "One-in-Ten Voters Online for Campaign '96," Washington, December 16, 1996.

Dirk Smillie, "News Breaks on the Web, But Can You Believe It?" *Christian Science Monitor,* October 1, 1997.

Paul Starobin, "On the Square," *National Journal,* May 25, 1996.

Rita Kirk Whillock, "Cyber-Politics," *American Behavioral Scientist,* vol. 40 (August 1997).

Debates (Format)

James A. Barnes, "The Debate over the Debates," *National Journal,* September 28, 1996.

David S. Broder, "Surviving on Sound Bites," *Washington Post*, October 23, 1996.

Don Hewitt, "Let's Have a Real Debate," *New York Times*, October 3, 1996.

Barbara Reynolds, "Who Gets In?" *Media Studies Journal*, vol. 11 (Winter 1997).

Alan Schroeder, "Watching between the Lines: Presidential Debates on Television," *Harvard International Journal of Press/Politics*, vol. 1 (Fall 1996).

Joel L. Swerdlow, ed., *Presidential Debates: 1988 and Beyond* (Washington: Congressional Quarterly Press, 1988).

Debates (News Coverage)

Roderick P. Hart and Sharon E. Jarvis, "Political Debates: Forms, Styles, and Media," *American Behavioral Scientist*, vol. 40 (August 1997).

Kathleen Hall Jamieson and David S. Birdsell, *Presidential Debates: The Challenge of Creating an Informed Electorate* (Oxford University Press, 1988).

Deborah Potter, "Wanted: Less Spin, More Substance," *Christian Science Monitor*, October 9, 1996.

Eleanor Randolph and Elizabeth Shogren, "Before, During and After, Journalists Get Full Spin Cycle," *Los Angeles Times*, October 7, 1996.

Twentieth Century Fund Task Force, *Let America Decide* (New York, 1995).

Disclosure

Alicia C. Shepard, "Talk is Expensive," *American Journalism Review* (May 1994).

————, "Take the Money and Talk," *American Journalism Review* (June 1995).

Election Night

James Barnes, "Election Night Heats Up—The Network Race to Make the Calls," *Public Perspective* (December–January 1997).

Curtis Gans, "Why Haley Barbour Should Sue Networks, Halt Vote Projections," *Roll Call*, October 28, 1996.

Howard Kurtz, "GOP Blasts Networks' Plan to Name Victor," *Washington Post*, October 30, 1996.

Lawrie Mifflin, "TV to Hold to Practice in Calling Election," *New York Times*, November 5, 1996.

Martha T. Moore, "Critics Believe TV Devalues Western Votes," *USA Today*, November 5, 1996.

Endorsements

Russell J. Dalton and others, "Partisan Cues and the Media: Information Flows in the 1992 Presidential Election," *American Political Science Review,* vol. 92 (March 1998).

Robert S. Erikson, "The Influence of Newspaper Endorsements in Presidential Elections: The Case of 1964," *American Journal of Political Science,* vol. 20 (May 1976).

Dorothy Giobbe, "Endorsement Enforcement," *Editor & Publisher*, April 6, 1996; and "Dole Wins . . . in Endorsements," *Editor & Publisher*, October 26, 1996.

John P. Robinson, "Perceived Media Bias and the 1968 Vote: Can the Media Affect Behavior After All?" *Journalism Quarterly*, vol. 49 (1974).

Michael Winerip, "At 'President McKinley's Paper,' the Editors Take Endorsements Seriously," *New York Times*, November 2, 1996.

Families

Karlyn Kohrs Campbell, *Shadowboxing with Stereotypes: The Press, the Public, and the Candidates' Wives,* research paper R-9, Shorenstein Center, Kennedy School, Harvard University, July 1993.

Kevin Merida and Susan Schmidt, "The Candidate's Wife and Partner in Climb," *Washington Post,* November 2, 1996.

Adam Nagourney, "Spouse on the Stump Faces New Role and New Scrutiny," *New York Times,* February 16, 1996.

Dennis F. Thompson, *Political Ethics and Public Office* (Harvard University Press, 1987).

Focus Groups

Andrew Ferguson, "The Focus-Group Fraud," *Weekly Standard,* October 14, 1996.

Warren Mitofsky, "Focus Groups: Uses, Abuses, and Misuses," *Harvard International Journal of Press/Politics,* vol. 1 (Spring 1996).

Stuart Rothenberg, "The Use and Misuse of Newest Polling Fad. Focus Groups," *Roll Call,* September 19, 1996.

Free TV

Christopher Adasiewicz and others, *Free Television for Presidential Candidates: The 1996 Experiment* (Annenberg Public Policy Center, University of Pennsylvania, 1997).

Marvin Kalb, "Free TV: More Time, Substance," *Washington Post,* March 20, 1996.

Thomas E. Mann and Norman J. Ornstein, "Credibility for a Collapsed System," *Washington Post,* December 16, 1996.

Paul Taylor, "Free TV Time Can Change Politics," *New York Daily News,* June 28, 1996.

Front Loading

David S. Broder, "Primary Madness," *Washington Post*, March 3, 1996.

Rhodes Cook, "GOP Wants a Revamp of Primary Process," *CQ*, August 9, 1997.

Alan Greenblatt and Rhodes Cook, "Nominating Process Rules Change," *CQ*, August 17, 1996.

William Safire, "Primary Reform Now," *New York Times*, March 28, 1996.

Gerald F. Seib, "Primary Issue: If It's Broke, Why Not Fix It?" *Wall Street Journal*, March 20, 1996.

Health

Herbert L. Abrams, "Presidential Health and the Public Interest: The Campaign of 1992," *Political Psychology*, vol. 10, no. 4 (1995).

George J. Annas, "The Health of the President and Presidential Candidates: The Public's Right to Know," *New England Journal of Medicine*, vol. 332 (October 5, 1995).

Robert H. Ferrell, *The Dying President: Franklin D. Roosevelt, 1944–1945* (University of Missouri Press, 1998).

Franz H. Messerli, "This Day 50 Years Ago," *New England Journal of Medicine*, vol. 333 (April 13, 1995).

Robert S. Robins and Jerrold M. Post, "Choosing a Healthy President," *Political Psychology*, vol. 16, no. 4 (1995).

Horse Race

"Take This Campaign—Please: TV News Coverage of the 1996 Presidential Election," *Media Monitor*, vol. 10, Center for Media and Public Affairs (September–October 1996).

Robert Lichter and Ted Smith, "Why Elections Are Bad News: Media and Candidate Discourse in the 1996 Presidential Primaries," *Harvard International Journal of Press/Politics*, vol. 1 (Fall 1996).

Walter R. Mears, "If the Campaign's a Horserace, Why Not Report It That Way?" *Nieman Reports,* vol. 49 (Winter 1995).

Graham P. Ramsden, "Media Coverage of Issues and Candidates: What Balance Is Appropriate in a Democracy?" *Political Science Quarterly,* vol. 111, no. 1 (1996).

Labels

L. Brent Bozell III, "Eroding Trust in Network News," *Washington Times,* March 22, 1996.

E. J. Dionne Jr., "The Labeling Games," *Washington Post Magazine,* August 11, 1996.

Doris A. Graber and David Weaver, "Presidential Performance Criteria: The Missing Element in Election Coverage," *Harvard International Journal of Press/Politics,* vol. 1 (Winter 1996).

Richard Harwood, "At a Loss for a Label," *Washington Post,* April 13, 1998.

Local TV News

Mark Fitzpatrick, "Local TV News Lacks Substance," *Editor & Publisher,* May 24, 1997.

Kaiser Family Foundation, *Assessing Local Television News Coverage of Health Issues* (Menlo Park, Calif., 1998).

Phyllis Kaniss, *Making Local News* (University of Chicago Press, 1991).

Paul Klite, "Local TV Newscasts Ignore Local Elections," *Television Quarterly,* vol. 28 (Fall 1996).

Barbara Bliss Osborn, "Election Neglected on L.A.'s Local TV," *Extra!,* vol. 10 (July–August 1997).

Steven D. Stark, "Local News: The Biggest Scandal on TV," *Washington Monthly,* June 1997.

Lying (for Journalists)

Russ Baker, "Damning Undercover Tactics as 'Fraud'," *Columbia Journalism Review* (March–April 1997).

James Boylan, "Punishing the Press," *Columbia Journalism Review* (March–April 1997).

Marvin Kalb, "Practicing Deception In the Pursuit of Truth," *Washington Post*, March 24, 1997.

Joan Konner, "The Truth About Lying," *Columbia Journalism Review* (May–June 1997).

Susan Paterno, "The Lying Game," *American Journalism Review,* vol. 29 (May 1997).

Lying (for Politicians)

Sissela Bok, *Lying: Moral Choice in Public and Private Life* (Pantheon, 1978).

Lisa Degliantoni, "Making Leaders and Mis-leaders," *Psychology Today,* vol. 29 (March 1996).

Stephen Hess, *The Government/Press Connection: Press Officers and Their Offices* (Brookings, 1984).

Anthony Marro, "When the Government Tells Lies," *Columbia Journalism Review* (March-April 1985).

Stuart Rothenberg, "Liar, Liar: Why Can't Politicians Talk Like Normal People Do?" *Roll Call*, June 5, 1997.

Metaphors

Carolyn Johnson, "Truce on War Metaphors," *PRNDI Newsletter*, Public Radio News Directors Incorporated, February 1996.

Margaret Scammell, "The Wisdom of the War Room: U.S. Campaigning and Americanization," research paper R-17, Shorenstein Center, Harvard University, April 1997.

Money

Howard Kurtz, "Alexander's Finances a Media Magnet," *Washington Post*, February 16, 1996.

Fred Wertheimer, "Forbes's Taxes are His Business," *New York Times*, February 13, 1996.

David Willman, "Tax Returns Show That Doles Are Millionaires," *Los Angeles Times*, January 20, 1996.

News Councils

Don Hewitt, "Mea Culpa? Not Mea!" *Wall Street Journal*, December 18, 1996.

Evan Jenkins, "News Councils: "The case for . . . and against," *Columbia Journalism Review* (March–April 1997).

John J. Oslund, "In Minneapolis: Ruling a Prizewinner Unfair," *Columbia Journalism Review* (March–April 1995).

Bob Shaw, "Minnesota News Council," http://www.mtn.org.

Alicia C. Shepard, "Going Public," *American Journalism Review* (April 1997).

Platforms

Jeff Fishel, *Presidents & Promises* (Washington: Congressional Quarterly Press, 1985).

Alan Greenblatt, "The Platform Dance," *CQ*, August 3, 1996.

Judith H. Parris, *The Convention Problem* (Brookings, 1972).

Gerald Pomper, with Susan Lederman, *Elections in America* (Dodd, Mead, 1976).

Polls (for Journalists)

James Bennet, "Polling Provoking Debate in News Media on Its Use," *New York Times*, October 4, 1996.

Kathleen A. Frankovic, "Public Opinion and Polling," in Doris Graber, Dennis McQuail, and Pippa Norris, eds., *The Politics of News, The News of Politics* (Washington: CQ Press, 1998).

John H. Fund, "The Perils of Polling," *Wall Street Journal*, August 13, 1996.

Andrew Gyory, "Poll-derol," *Forbes MediaCritic*, vol. 3 (Summer 1996).

Lawrence R. Jacobs and Robert Y. Shapiro, "The Polling Crisis," *Roll Call*, April 28, 1997.

Michael R. Kagay, "Experts Say Refinements Are Needed in the Polls," *New York Times*, December 15, 1996.

Paul J. Lavrakas, Michael W. Traugott, and Peter V. Miller, eds., *Presidential Polls and the News Media* (Boulder, Colo.: Westview Press, 1995).

Thomas E. Mann and Gary R. Orren, editors, *Media Polls in American Politics* (Brookings, 1992).

Polls (for Politicians)

Michael K. Frisby, "Clinton Seeks Strategic Edge with Opinion Polls," *Wall Street Journal*, June 24, 1996.

Albert R. Hunt, "The Reich Question: Where Is Clinton's Core?" *Wall Street Journal*, April 3, 1997.

Dick Morris, *Behind the Oval Office* (Random House, 1997).

William Schneider, "Here's One High-Stakes Numbers Game," *National Journal*, May 3, 1997.

Predictions

Albert Eisele, "Expecting the Unexpected," *The Hill*, June 5, 1996.

Howard Kurtz, "Prediction Addiction," *Forbes MediaCritic*, vol. 3 (Summer 1996).

Suzan Revah, "Forecast for the Political Crystal Ball: Cloudy," *American Journalism Review,* vol. 18 (July–August 1996).

Lee Sigelman, Jarol B. Manheim, and Susannah Pierce, "Inside Dopes? Pundits as Political Forecasters," *Harvard International Journal of Press/Politics,* vol. 1 (Winter 1996).

Push Polls

Adam Clymer, "Phony Polls That Sling Mud Raise Questions over Ethics," *New York Times,* May 20, 1996.

Mac Hansbrough, "Dial N for Negative," *Campaigns and Elections,* vol. 13 (April 1992).

Larry J. Sabato and Glenn R. Simpson, *Dirty Little Secrets: The Persistence of Corruption in American Politics* (Times Books, 1996).

Revolving Door

Suzanne Fields, "News That Entertains," *Washington Times,* July 24, 1997.

Max Frankel, "Something Doesn't Love a Wall," *New York Times Magazine,* January 19, 1997.

Carl T. Rowan, "'In and Out' Journalists," *Washington Post,* December 21, 1988.

William Safire, "Color Me Tainted," *New York Times,* December 12, 1988.

Alicia C. Shepard, "The Revolving Door," *American Journalism Review,* vol. 19 (July–August 1997).

Charles Trueheart, "Trading Places," *Washington Post,* January 4, 1989.

Lewis W. Wolfson, "Through the Revolving Door," research paper R-4, Shorenstein Center, Harvard University, June 1991.

Sex Scandals

Sisscla Bok, "School for Scandal," discussion paper D-4, Shorenstein Center, Harvard University, April 1990.

The Little Book of Campaign Etiquette

Max Frankel, "To Pry or Not to Pry?" *New York Times Magazine*, November 3, 1996.

Suzanne Garment, *Scandal: The Culture of Mistrust in American Politics* (Times Books, 1991).

Susan Paterno, "An Affair to Ignore," *American Journalism Review* (January–February 1997).

Jonathan Rauch, "Live and Let Live," *New Republic*, September 22, 1997.

Larry Sabato, *Feeding Frenzy* (Free Press, 1991).

Gerald F. Seib, "2000 Quandary: Private Lives, Public Campaign," *Wall Street Journal*, April 22, 1998.

Sound Bites

Kiku Adatto, *Picture Perfect: The Art and Artifice of Public Image Making* (Basic Books, 1993).

Lamar Alexander, "Let Us Speak for Ourselves," *Media Studies Journal*, vol. 11 (Winter 1997).

Daniel C. Hallin, "Sound Bite News: Television Coverage of Elections, 1968–1988," *Journal of Communication*, vol. 42 (1992).

Catherine A. Steele and Kevin G. Barnhurst, "The Journalism of Opinion: Network News Coverage of U.S. Presidential Campaigns, 1968–1988," *Critical Studies in Mass Communication*, vol. 13 (September 1996).

Mitchell Stephens, "On Shrinking Soundbites," *Columbia Journalism Review* (September–October 1996).

Straw Polls

Emmett H. Buell Jr., "The Invisible Primary," in William G. Mayer, ed., *In Pursuit of the White House: How We Choose Our Presidential Nominees* (Chatham, N.J.: Chatham House, 1996).

Talk Radio

Ann Devroy, "Clinton Foes Voice Their Hostility Loud and Clear," *Washington Post*, May 22, 1994.

Timothy Egan, "Triumph Leaves No Targets for Conservative Talk Shows," *New York Times*, January 1, 1995.

Ronald D. Elving, "On Radio, All Politics Is a Lot Less Vocal," *CQ*, May 10, 1997.

Robert LaFranco, "Radio Redux," *Forbes*, April 11, 1994.

Brian Lehrer, "I Doubt Media 'Cult of Certainty,' " *New York Daily News*, May 13, 1997.

Voters

Stephen Ansolabehere, Shanto Iyengar, Adam Simon, and Nicholas Vantentino, "Does Attack Advertising Demobilize the Electorate?" *American Political Science Review*, vol. 88 (December 1994).

Eliza Newlin Carney, "Options out of Politics," *National Journal*, January 17, 1998.

Curtis Gans, "In Search of the Citizen," *Roll Call*, October 24, 1996.

Jack W. Germond and Jules Witcover, "Why Americans Don't Go to the Polls," *National Journal*, November 23, 1996.

Peter F. Nardulli, Jon K. Dalager, and Donald E. Greco, "Voter Turnout in U.S. Presidential Elections: An Historical View and Some Speculation," *PS:Political Science & Politics*, vol. 29 (September 1996).

Daniel Sneider, "Do Lower Voter Turnouts Show Contempt? Or Contentment?" *Christian Science Monitor*, November 6, 1996.

Ruy A. Teixeira, *The Disappearing American Voter* (Brookings, 1992).

Winning & Losing

Paul E. Corcoran, "Presidential Concession Speeches: The Rhetoric of Defeat," *Political Communication*, vol. 11 (June 1994).